## How to arrive to the principal places of Paris via Metro or RER

| Destination | Line | Station |
|---|---|---|
| Arc de Triomphe | A, 1, 2, 3 | Ch. de Gaulle-Étoile |
| Bastille | 1, 5, 8 | Bastille |
| Beaubourg | 1, 11 | Hôtel de Ville |
| | 11 | Rambuteau |
| Champ-de-Mars | 8 | École Militaire |
| Champs-Élysées | 1 | George V |
| | 1, 13, | Champs-Élysées-Clemenceau |
| | 1, 9 | Franklin D. Roosevelt |
| Cimetière du Père-Lachaise | 2, 3 | Père-Lachaise |
| | 3, 3 bis | Gambetta |
| Conciergerie | 4 | Cité |
| | B, C | St-Michel-Notre-Dame |
| Défense | 1 | Esplanade de la Défense |
| | A | La Défense *Grande Arche* |
| Forum des Halles | 4 | Les Halles |
| | A, B, D | Châtelet-les Halles |
| Grand Palais | 1, 13 | Champs-Élysées-Clemenceau |
| Hôtel de Ville | 1, 11 | Hôtel de Ville |
| Île St-Louis | 7 | Pont Marie |
| Invalides | 8 | École Militaire |
| | C, 8, 13 | Invalides |
| Luxembourg | 4 - 10 | Odéon |
| | B | Luxembourg |
| Madeleine | 8, 12, 14 | Madeleine |
| Montmartre | 12 | Abbesses |
| | 2 | Blanche |
| Montparnasse | 4 | Vavin |
| Musée Carnavalet | 1 | St-Paul |
| | 8 | Chemin Vert |
| Musée d'Orsay | C | Musée d'Orsay |
| Musée du Louvre | 1, 7 | Palais Royal-Musée du Louvre |
| Notre-Dame | 4 | Cité |
| | B, C | St-Michel-Notre-Dame |
| Opéra | 3, 7, 8 | Opéra |
| Palais Royal | 1, 7 | Palais Royal-Musée du Louvre |
| Panthéon | B | Luxembourg |
| Petit Palais | 1, 13 | Champs-Élysées-Clemenceau |
| Place de la Concorde | 1, 8, 12 | Concorde |
| Place Vendôme | 3, 7, 8 | Opéra |
| Rue de Rivoli | 1, 8, 12 | Concorde |
| | 1 | Louvre-Rivoli |
| Sacré-Cœur | 12 | Abbesses |
| Sorbonne | 4 - 10 | Odéon |
| | 10 | Maubert Mutualité |
| Ste-Chapelle | 4 | Cité |
| St-Eustache | 4 | Les Halles |
| | A, B, D | Châtelet-Les Halles |
| St-Sulpice | 4 | St-Sulpice |
| | 10 | Mabillon |
| Tour Eiffel | C | Champ-de-Mars-Tour Eiffel |
| | 6 | Bir hakeem |
| Versailles | C5 | Versailles-Rive Gauche *Château de Versailles* |

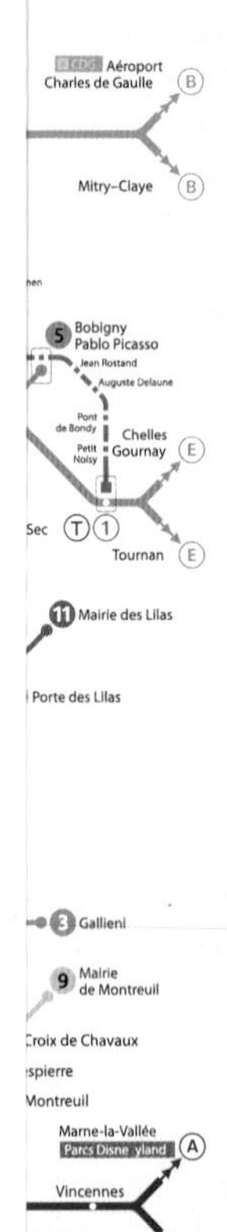

# *the guide of Paris*

http://www.paravision.org
info@paravision.org

Summary

## IV. Visit itineraries in Paris

# I A BRIEF HISTORICAL BACKGROUND

A human presence has been detected in Paris as far as the fifth millenary B.C. This fact was attested by bones of cervidae and reindeers hunted by men and dating back to that epoch which were discovered in 1886 in a quarry at Beaugrenelle.

Traces of rural settlement and Neolithic tombs were also unearthed at the Louvre courtyards during the excavations undertaken at the beginning of the XXth century.

The first sedentary inhabitants of Paris were itinerant hunters who decided to settle in the city because of its temperate climate as well as the presence of the Seine. This river offered a natural refuge on the « Île de la Cité » which became over the years the historic heart of the capital.

The Seine river also offered the possibility of touring by boat around a large perimeter, and provided the advantage of being navigable all year round. Hence, commercial exchange rapidly grew, and Paris became an important river crossroads.

*>> The Seine*

**The first true « Parisians »** were members of a Gallic tribe of the name « Parisii ». They settled in Paris around 250 B.C., thus succeeding to the Celts who were the first historic inhabitants.
At that epoch, Paris was known as « Lutèce » (Lutetia), and became a real place of exchange through which transited products and goods coming from the vast Roman Empire. Afterwards, Lutetia became known as « the town of the Parisii », before acquiring its final designation « Paris » in the 5th century A.D.
In 52 B.C., the Romans conquered Lutetia and the proconsul Labienus was in charge of administering the city. He engaged in a policy of tolerance with regards to religious matters and planned to turn Lutetia into a major commercial axis for the Empire. Hence, a period of peaceful cohabitation between the Gaul people and the Romans lasts for several centuries. Few vestiges of the ancient Gallo-Roman city remain, only the ancient Thermes of Paris (public baths) are still visible at the level of the Musée du Moyen-Âge (Museum of the Middle Ages), at Rue de Cluny.
With the **fall of the Roman Empire in** 476, the population of Paris lost its protector. When Attila, known as God's Curse, threatened Paris in 451, a young woman named Genevieve asked the Parisians not to escape, but rather pray. Facing the wrath and menaces of the most frightened, Genevieve remained firm as she had seen in her dreams that Paris would not be destroyed. The Parisians did not escape and the prediction of Saint Genevieve proved to be

>> *The Roman Baths of Cluny*

>> *The Pantheon*

true : the Huns headed towards Orleans and were defeated at the Catalonian battlefields. Henceforth, everybody came asking the help of the former shepherdess.

Later on, she saved Paris against other barbarians coming from the East, the Franks, by providing ammunitions to the besieged, which earned her the title of patron saint of Paris. Hence, mount Saint-Genevieve in Paris, towered over by the Pantheon today, evokes her memory.

Clovis, King of the Franks, ends up conquering the city in 508, along with a vast area which will become later on the state of « France ». He chooses to settle in Paris to rule his kingdom and decides to convert to Christianity by getting baptized. By doing so, the Franks stand out from the other Barbarians and get the support of the Gallo-Roman clergy. Moreover, Clovis decides to be buried in Paris, next to Saint-Genevieve, in the Basilica of Saint-Denis, north of Paris. His descendants, the Merovingians, continue to consider Paris as their main city.

The Carolingians succeed to the Merovingians as of 751 A.D. Since they have eastern origins, from the Rhine surroundings, the center of power moves to Metz, then to Aix-La-Chapelle. Nonetheless, Carolingian Kings, with the exception of Charlemagne, maintain the tradition of getting inhumed at Saint Denis, where all the kings of Paris shall be buried from then on.

When Gozlin, the abbot of Saint-Denis nominates Eudes, son of Robert le Fort, as Count of Paris in 882, the power of the Carolingians is undermined by a second wave of invasions of Viking and Hungarian origins. Eudes wins his fame by defending Paris, besieged by the Normans. Although he was not a Carolingian, the Nobles of the kingdom chose Eudes to become the king of occidental France in 888, because he proved to be an intrepid leader in his fight against the Normans. The occidental France expands to the territories occupied by the Franks and situated to the west of the Meuse, i.e. almost the Northern part of the current France ●

In 987, Eudes' great-grandson, **Hughes Capet**, becomes king of France. He founds the Capetian dynasty whose reign will last until Louis-Philippe, last king of France who will abdicate the throne in 1848 after three days of riots.

Paris truly becomes the **capital of France** in the XIIth century, through the impetus given by the first Capetians who decide to build some constructions symbolizing the attachment of their dynasty to the city. Hence, from 1190 to 1202, king Philippe-Auguste builds the medieval castle of the Louvre, which shall be transformed into the current museum, thus fulfilling his wish of turning this city into his own capital.

Later on, Saint-Louis also initiates the building of the Sainte-Chapelle from 1243 until 1248, where he places the Christ's crown of thorns that the Emperor of Constantinople had given him. With the Notre Dame Cathedral built between 1163 and 1270, this combination altogether forms a unique artistic and religious setting, in the heart of Paris.

The city expands throughout the Middle Ages and becomes the largest town in France. At the end of this period, Paris acquires an exceptional size and importance in the kingdom and constitutes with Naples the largest city in Europe with 200,000 inhabitants.

*>> Notre-Dame de Paris*

**François I**, son of Charles de Valois-Orléans, Count of Angoulême, and Louise de Savoie, succeeds to his cousin and father-in-law Louis XII in 1515. After leading the « wars of Italy », François I decides to draw his inspiration from the art of the « Italian Renaissance ».

>> *The Louvre construction*

With this spirit, he starts the works at the Louvre. First of all, he orders the demolition of the central dungeon in 1528, leaving the space for a big central courtyard. Then he commissions the architect Pierre Lescot to perform some major modifications in 1546 in order to build a modern palace.

François I also founds the « Collège de France » in the Latin Quarter. The construction of a Hôtel de Ville is also scheduled; however, it shall not be completed until the reign of Henri IV more than 50 years later.

**Henri II**, son of François I, carries on the works at the Louvre. He resides at the Hôtel des Tournelles awaiting their completion. After the injury of Henri II by Montgomery during a tournament which leads to his death, Catherine of Medicis orders the demolition of the Hôtel des Tournelles. Thus, she decides to reside at the Louvre with her children and commissions the building of an even bigger palace, on the western side of the Louvre, « the Tuileries », based on the designs of architects Philippe Delorme and Jean Bullant.

Under the rule of Henri II, Pierre Lescot and the sculptor Jean Gougeon erect the « Fontaine des Innocents » (Fountain of the Innocents) conceived under the shape of an altar dedicated to the nymphs. At the heart of what used to be a medieval quarter in the XVIth century, where life and death met on a daily basis, this fountain symbolized the spirit of the Renaissance.

During this epoch, the draining of the Marais quarter is undertaken, where a particular hotel is constructed for the President of Parliament. This hotel hosts today the « Musée Carnavalet », as well as the churches Saint-Etienne du Mont situated near the current Pantheon and Saint-Eustache which is in the vicinity of Les Halles.

This period shall also be marked by the « wars of religions », opposing Catholics against Protestants. Its peak is the night of « Saint Bartholomew », on August 24, 1572, where many Protestants are massacred in Paris.
Situated west of Paris, the Château of Saint-Germain-en-Laye also undergoes some important extension works during the same epoch, thus reaching an area of 8,000

*>> The night of «Saint Bartholomew»*

square meters in 1559. In 1578, Henri III starts off the construction works of the « Pont Neuf » (New Bridge) which would be the first bridge not surrounded by houses. The construction works of this bridge, today the oldest bridge in Paris, as well as the Hôtel de Ville are completed under the reign of Henri IV.

>> The «Paiais du Louvre»

Upon his arrival to Paris in 1594, **Henri IV** decides to join the Louvre and the Tuileries forming a gigantic palace. Hence, he starts implementing the first phase of his « Grand Dessein » (Great Scheme), the « Grande Galerie du bord de l'eau » (Great gallery bordering the water).

>> The Tuileries

The quays of the Seine are laid out, the sewers are dug out, and the number of pumps is increased, amongst which the one known as the « Samaritaine » that owes its name to the statue decorating it on a stack at the Pont Neuf. Nearby, at the western end of the Île de la Cité, the « Place Dauphine » (Dauphine square) is situated, in honor of the Dauphin, the future Louis XIII.

>> *The Pont Neuf*

Over the ruins of the Hôtel des Tournelles, Henri IV decides to build the « Place Royale » (Royal Square), today designated as the Place des Vosges. This Square is completed in 1612 thus the Marais becomes a fashionable quarter housing sumptuous hotels in a style « à la français » where the exhibitions are held •

>> *The «Place des Vosges»*

In 1615, **Marie of Medicis**, mother of the future king Louis XIII, assigns the architect Salomon de Brosse to build the « Palais du Luxembourg » (Luxembourg Palace). She resides at the palace as of the year 1625, but is forced to leave on the year of completion of works by order of her son Louis XIII, after the episode known as the « Journée des dupes ».

**Cardinal Richelieu** commissions the architect Le Mercier to build the « Palais Cardinal » (Cardinal Palace) in the vicinity of the Louvre, which ownership shall go back to the crown upon the Cardinal's death; hence its name becomes the « Palais Royal ». Richelieu also launches the building of the Sorbonne church, with a cupola inspired by Saint-Peter of Rome, under which his tomb is placed.

>> *«Palais Royal»*

In 1626, **Louis XIII** decides to set up a « Royal garden of medicinal plants » near the Latin Quarter, designated today as the « Jardin des plantes » (Botanical Garden).

The area of Paris is yet enlarged by the young king who also unites the two islets, near the Île de la Cité, which become the Île Saint-Louis joined to the right bank by the construction of a new bridge, the « Pont Marie ».

After the king's death in 1643, a civil war called the « Fronde », is triggered off under the regency of **Anne of Austria**. This insurrection obliges the royal family to flee from Paris, which explains the distrust of **Louis XIV** later on vis-à-vis the Parisians. This shall be one of the reasons that compel him to reside in Versailles.

Louis XIV seldom lives in Paris, even before residing in Versailles. The « Sun King » does not however neglect the city which already has five hundred thousand inhabitants. Hence, he engages in some important reconstruction works, namely through the demolition of the fortifications that had become almost unnecessary; instead they are replaced by boulevards.

In fact, the center of Paris has undergone little change since the Middle Ages; however, the city extends particularly to the right bank. The lighting

>> *The «Palais du Luxembourg»*

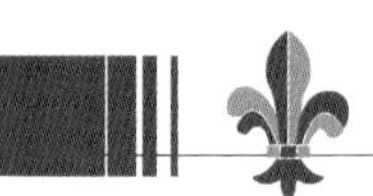

of the streets improves as well as the work of the Parisian police, created by La Reynie. In 1664, **Colbert**, the great minister of Louis XIV, orders the construction of the « Manufacture royale des Gobelins » (Parisian Tapestry Manufactory) on the borders of the Bièvre river. It shall be named later on the « Manufacture royale des meubles et tapisseries de la couronne » (Royal manufacture of furniture and tapestries of the crown).

The landscape architect Le Nôtre draws the plans of the Tuileries Garden and the Champs Elysées. At the same time, the Louvre continues to expand and Claude Perrault endows it with a magnificent Colonnade. This talented architect also builds the Observatoire (Observatory).

**Cardinal Mazarin**, former Prime Minister of the Regent Anne of Austria, shall be in charge of the education of Louis XIV thus accumulating a colossal fortune. Upon his death, Mazarin bequeaths a large sum of money to build a School, constructed by Le Vau, which will later on be named « Bibliothèque Mazarine » before becoming the « Institut de France », headquarter of the five academies.

*>> Louis XIV*

A hospital, « la Salpêtrière », is also built during the same epoch to take in abandoned children as well as sick women and disabled people. On the left bank, Louis XIV appoints Mansart to erect the « Hôtel des Invalides » destined to take in mutilated soldiers. The coffin of Emperor Napoleon 1st rests under its dome since 1840.

Under the reign of Louis XIV, triumphal arches are erected at Portes

>> «Le Champs de Mars »

Saint-Denis and Saint-Martin in his honor. At this epoch, the squares of place des Victoires and place Vendôme which comprise statues of Louis XIV at their center as well as numerous private mansions are built, especially in the new quarters in the periphery of Paris.

Towards the end of Louis XIV's reign, who dies in 1711, signs of boredom somewhat start to show in Versailles. Hence, numerous noblemen begin constructing rich mansions, particularly in the suburbs of Faubourg Saint-Germain and Saint-Honoré, among which the Bourbon palace-which hosts today the Assemblée Nationale (National Assembly) - and the Palais de l'Elysée, which is since 1873 the residence of the Presidents of the Republic.

Under the reign of **Louis XV**, the « Ecole Militaire » (military school) is built. It is aimed at training 500 students of modest origins to become officers. The architect Jacques-Ange Gabriel erects this edifice between 1751 and 1768 at the Beaugrenelle plain, next to the Invalides, while building a vast parade ground, the « Champ de Mars ». The school which becomes in 1777 the « Ecole des Cadets Gentilhommes » had amongst its students the young Napoleon Bonaparte in 1784. The military school takes in today the « Collège inter-armée » (inter-army school).

Gabriel also draws the plans of square Louis XV, which is the current place de la Concorde, around

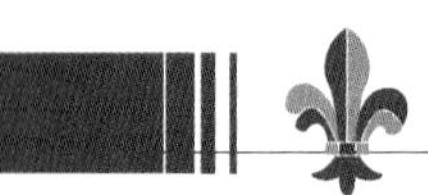

>> *The Crillon hotel and the Ministry of the Navy*

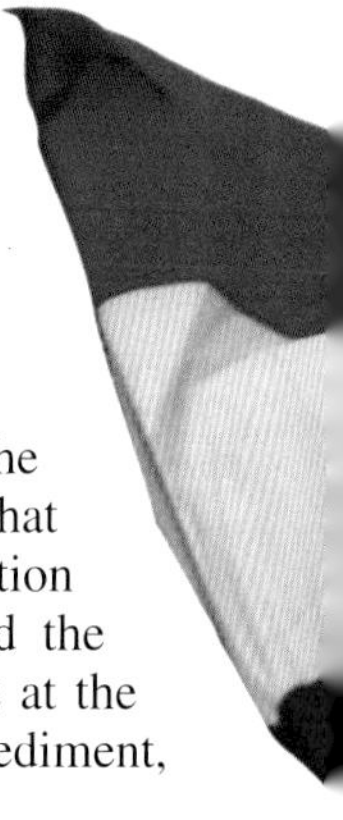

which two magnificent private mansions are erected, symbolizing the architectural style of that epoch. These buildings embrace today the Crillon hotel and the Ministry of the Navy.

The Medical School situated in the Latin Quarter and the Veterinary School of Maisons-Alfort also date back to that epoch. Moreover, during this same period, the construction works of the church Saint-Sulpice are under way, and the construction of a new church of Saint-Genevieve begins at the same location of the old one, with a dome and a pediment, according to the designs of the architect Soufflot.

The old Regime also witnesses the construction of the Hôtel des Monnaies on the quay Conti, as well as the Royal Manufacture of porcelain of Sèvres •

**Louis XVI**, grand-son of Louis VX, is king of France from 1774 to 1791. Under his rule, the Comédie Française is built, which was conceived by Louis XIV, and so is the case of Odéon Theater and the Louis XVI Bridge, which links up the square Louis XV to the Faubourg Saint-Germain today known as the Pont de la Concorde.

The center of Paris is renovated as well during the same epoch. Consequently, the houses built on the bridges are demolished, the cemetery of the Innocents is razed for hygienic reasons and the bones are transferred to the « Catacombs ».

The reign of Louis XVI also witnesses the construction of the « enceinte des Fermiers Généraux » (the enclosure of the Fermiers Généraux). The latter are in charge of collecting taxes; hence the project is aimed at establishing city toll pavilions to collect entrance fees on merchandises coming into Paris. Today, all what remains of these constructions are the « Barrière d'Enfer » (hell barrier), « Barrière du Trône » (Throne barrier), and the « Rotonde de la Villette » (Rotunda of La Villette).

The Palais-Royal (Royal palace), owned by the Duc d'Orléans, cousin of the King, is outfitted with new buildings and arcade shaped galleries bordering the garden which becomes the meeting point of elegant people, and later on, the ferment of the Revolution ideas.

*>> The French flag, created during the Revolution*

The influence of Paris, intellectual and cultural capital of Europe, reached its peak in the XVIIIth century. Literary and artistic life flourished in churches due to baroque music namely in theaters such as the Odeon, which is today the Comédie-Française. Concepts of encyclopaedists were largely diffused in the salons, such as those of Madame de Tencin, Madame Geoffrin or Madame de Lambert as well as in cafés which abounded, the most famous being Le Procope.

In July 1789, **the Revolution** starts in Paris and the Bastille, symbol of royal power, is conquered and demolished. In August 1792, after the storming of the Tuileries, the royal

family is imprisoned in the dungeon of the Temple's fortress, built in the XIIIth century by the Templars and demolished in 1811.
From 1792 until 1794, France is governed by an Assembly that bears the name of the « Convention ». Its leaders decide to transform the Louvre into a Museum, they establish the Muséum d'Histoire Naturelle (Museum of Natural History), the École Normale Supérieure to train teachers (Grande École for training of teachers), and the École Polytechnique to train engineers and officers. The École des Langues Orientales (School of Oriental Languages) is also established at this epoch, as well as the National Conservatoire of Arts and Crafts and the Conservatoire de Musique et Déclamation (Paris Conservatoire).
As to the Royal Libraries, they are grouped in the old Hôtel Mazarin, under the name « Bibliothèque Nationale » (French national library).
At the end of the century, Paris is divided into twelve « arrondissements » (districts) by the Directoire (Directory), which is the name of the government at that epoch.
On November 9, 1799, General Napoleon Bonaparte puts en end to the régime of the « Directoire » and paves the way for a new régime by ending the revolution itself. From there on, life regains its normal course in Paris and big construction projects are initiated.
The Bank of France is created, in an ancient hotel of the peculiar XVIIth century, as well as the Palais de la Légion d'Honneur in an ancient hotel of the peculiar XVIIIth century.
The construction of the Arc de Triomphe (Triumph Arch) of the Etoile is undertaken, as well as the Colonne Vendôme, the Temple de

*>> The Arc de Triomphe, Place de l'Étoile*

la Gloire (Temple of Glory)-the church of La Madelaine today - and the Bourse (Stock Exchange).
In 1808, Napoleon I, already an Emperor, asks his architects Charles Percier and Pierre Fontaine to erect, between the Louvre and the Tuileries, an arch of triumph for the glory of the Grande Armée (Great Army), the arch of triumph of the Carrousel.
At the same time, new streets are opened up and two new bridges are built. The Halle aux vins (wine market) is also established, and the construction of the canal Saint-Martin (Saint-Martin's channel) starts at this epoch.
At the outskirts of the city, the Cimetières (Cemeteries) of Montmartre, of Père Lachaise and Montparnasse are built.
A Restoration period succeeds to the First Empire and witnesses the reign of **Louis XVIII** and **Charles X**. During their rule, the royal statues are restored, among which that of Henri IV on the Pont Neuf. Also, the constructions initiated during Napoleon's rule carry on. Lines of omnibus drawn by horses are established, as well as two new bridges, and gas lighting of the streets starts.

*>> Le Pont Saint-Michel*

*>> The Obelisk, Place de la Concorde*

Under the reign of **Louis-Philippe**, from 1830 to 1848, the Obelisk of Egypt's Pasha offered to Charles X is erected at Concorde square. Numerous monuments are restored and the Versailles Palace is rescued from ruin. At the location of the Bastille, the « Colonne de Juillet » is erected in memory of revolutionary days that overthrew Charles X from the throne.

>> *The ashes of Napoleon Bonaparte are deposited in the Invalides*

In 1840, England grants king Louis-Philippe the retrieval of the ashes of Napoleon I which he transfers under the dome of the Invalides.

Two new bridges are once more built, and it is the inception of the railway with the creation of the « Gares du Nord » (Rail Stations of the North), of the East, of Montparnasse, and of Lyon.

Paris has almost one million inhabitants under Louis-Philippe's reign. He decides to protect the city by a new fortified fence of 34 kilometers length, comprising 16 forts. This fortification is demolished later on; it is now replaced by the boulevards known as the « Maréchaux » (Marshals), since they bear the names of the Empire's Marshals.

Under the Second Empire, **Napoleon III** entrusts **Haussmann** with the endeavor of developing Paris. Thus, big construction works are initiated which will completely remodel the Capital's aspect and indisputably embellish it.

Large arteries are opened up or completed : the boulevards of Strasbourg, Sébastopol, Saint-Michel, Saint-Germain, Prince Eugène (today known as Voltaire), Magenta, Malesherbes, Haussmann, as well as the streets Saint-Denis, Saint-Martin, Saint-Jacques, Rivoli…

On the other hand, old houses are torn down, new constructions are regulated, the square of the Hôtel de Ville is widened, and the Palais Royal is refurbished.

>> *The axes of Paris by Haussmann*

In 1852, Napoleon III decides to add a new extension to the Louvre palace surrounding a vast U shaped courtyard - the Napoleon courtyard-prolonged by two wings parallel to the Seine River on the south and to Rue de Rivoli on the north. During this epoch, the Pavillon de Flore is also built, at the tip of the southern wing.

During the same epoch, architect Baltard builds the central Halles (market). Two new bridges stride across the Seine, the Saint-Michel fountain is erected and Garnier puts up the Opera, which now bears his name.

Under the Second Empire, the theaters of Châtelet and la Ville are also erected; the Bois de Boulogne and de Vincennes are built, as well as numerous other squares. Moreover, the parks of Buttes Chaumont and Montsouris are created. This period also witnesses the start up of the first « Grands Magasins » (department stores).

In 1860, 13 Communes are incorporated into Paris. The city is then divided into 20 arrondissements (districts) and comprises one million and a half inhabitants.

After the defeat of 1870 against Prussia, the Republic is proclaimed anew. The French Government which retreated to Versailles has to face the « Commune », an insurrection triggered in Paris. The « Versaillees » retrieve Paris, but in the course of the battles, the Tuileries, the Palais Royal and the Hôtel de Ville are set on fire, and the Colonne Vendôme knocked down. The latter shall stand up again, The Palais Royal shall be restored, the Hôtel de Ville rebuilt, however, the Tuileries deemed as too damaged shall be razed.

*>> The Basilica of the Sacré-Coeur*

>> *The Eiffel Tower seen from the Trocadero*

In 1875, the construction of the Basilica of the Sacré-Coeur (Sacred Heart) is undertaken on top of the Montmartre hill. At the same time, the existing rail stations are expanded and the Gare d'Orsay (Orsay railway) is built up, which is today a Museum bearing the same name. Works for the construction of the Metro are also initiated based on the designs of the engineer Bienvenue.

In the prospect of the Exposition Universelle (World Fair) of 1878, the Palais du Trocadéro and the Tour Eiffel are erected, the latter named after its engineer Gustave Eiffel. Also the construction of the Alexander III Bridge is undertaken in honor of the Tsar of Russia.

Towards the end of the XIXth century and the beginning of the XXth, the World Fairs that take place in Paris induce the City to create the « Grand et Petit Palais » (Great and Small Palace), which will later on be fitted out into Museums for temporary or permanent exhibitions.

After the war of 1914-1918, an unknown soldier is buried under the Arc de Triomphe of the Etoile on November 11, 1920, anniversary of the Armistice of 1918.

For the World Fair of 1937, the Trocadero is demolished and replaced by the Palais de Chaillot, on the hill bearing the same name.

>> *The plaque of Charles de Gaulle's statue*

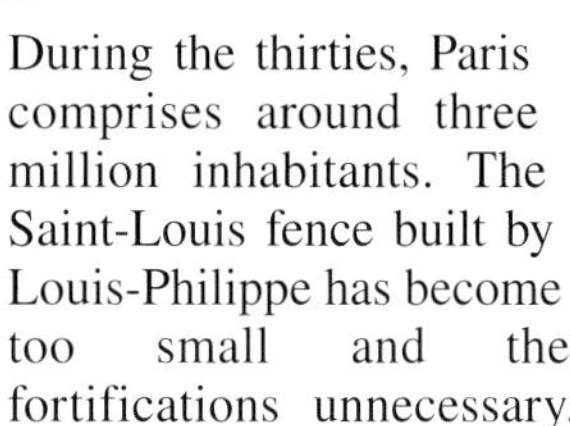

During the thirties, Paris comprises around three million inhabitants. The Saint-Louis fence built by Louis-Philippe has become too small and the fortifications unnecessary. Therefore, these are wrecked and replaced by boulevards.

However, the Second World War and the German occupation shall temporarily interrupt the development of the city.

As of the second half of the XXth century, Paris shall undergo yet another transformation. The construction of a large business center is initiated at La Défense. Les Halles, too small and poorly situated due to the growth of automobile traffic, are transferred to the South-East of Paris, in Rungis. A vast underground complex is built at their old location, topped by a garden, the Forum. Nearby, Pompidou Center, a museum of modern art, is built on the plateau Beaubourg.

On the border of the Seine, at the left bank, the modern Institut du Monde Arabe (Institute of the Arab World) is inaugurated in 1987. A vast Opera house is also erected at Place de la Bastille (Bastille square) and inaugurated in 1989. At the Villette, instead of the old abattoirs (slaughterhouses), the Cité des Sciences (City of Sciences) and the Cité de la Musique (City of Music) are built.

In the early nineties, towards the old Halle aux Vins in Bercy, the new Ministry of Finance and the Grande Bibliothèque de France (Great Library of France) are built, the latter aimed at substituting the historical National Library of the Richelieu street •

# .2.
# Parisian Gastronomy,
## A Historic Tradition

## II PARISIAN GASTRONOMY

### A HISTORIC TRADITION

*Paris, the capital of gastronomy.*

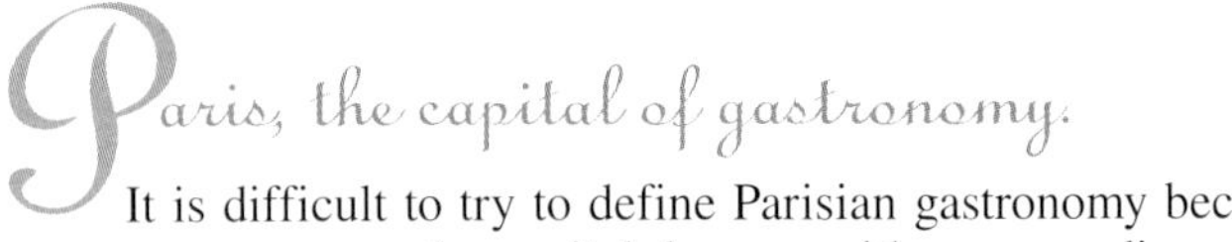

It is difficult to try to define Parisian gastronomy because the capital devours with gourmandise wines and exotic delicacies. However, it is in the bakery that one really feels the beating heart of the capital. Cradle of the « baguette » which was invented in the XVIth century, it will migrate to the province only towards the middle of the XXth century. As to Parisian patisserie, it exalts light pastes and embraces evocative names such as « Saint-Honoré », « Paris-Brest », or « Opéra ». It is also adorned in nobleness and tradition, much like the famous « macarons » of the « Ladurée » shop at rue Royale since 1867…

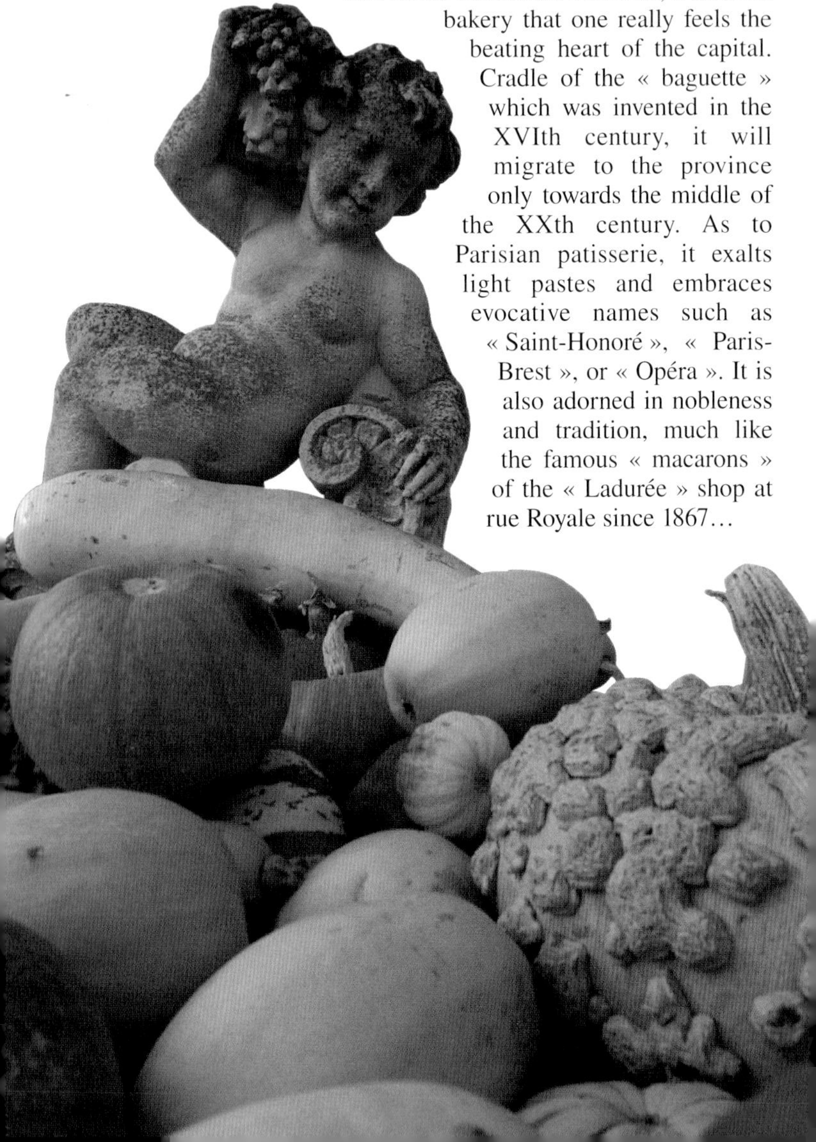

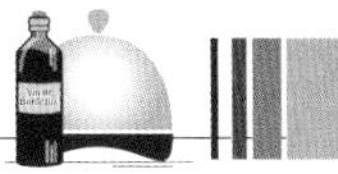

From a historical viewpoint, the real boom in French and Parisian cuisine takes place during the reign of the absolute and centralist monarchy, which reached its peak under **Louis XIV** in the XVIIth century in Versailles.

At that epoch, the one-upmanship in dishes and preparations is a reflection of the pyramid-like structure of politics, with the Sun King installed at the top. Thus, lavish meals, stage-managed to great effect, become a means of glorifying the sovereign.

The reign of Louis XIV, from 1643 to 1715 established the importance of « etiquette » which represents the set of rules defining the procedures and hierarchies in force at the court as well as good wining and dining.

In this context, the **Duke of Saint-Simon**, chronicler of life at the court, pays tribute to this monarch with the vast appetite, who encourages service in the French manner, thus all the dishes are served at the same time, with guests arranged around the table according to a precise table plan, to which the Sun King adds an unbelievable amount of decorum. Hence, Saint-Simon writes about Louis XIV : « In everything he loved splendor, magnificence, profusion. This taste, he turned it into maxims through politics, and inspired him in everything at his court ».

In 1651, **La Varenne** publishes his work « Le Cuisinier français », which introduces a new conception of culinary art. One hundred thousand copies of this book are printed, which constitutes a record at that epoch!

As to **François Massialot**, he structures the recipes and proposes a French model transposable to the dining rooms of the middle-classes and foreign courts, namely through his renowned book « Cuisinier Royal et Bourgeois », published in 1691.

According to **Anthony Rowley**, author of the book « A table ! », there is no doubt that Louis XIV bestowed on gastronomy its national supremacy. He is also responsible for cultivating the art of conversation at table. As a matter of fact, in France, people appreciate not only the pleasures of fine dining but also that of talking about it, a practice that often surprises foreign visitors.

Under the old regime, the Court of France is the crucible for

« la Grande Cuisine », with dining becoming a means of government and of exercising political influence. That was the case for instance during the amazing banquet given by **François I** in 1520, at the Field of the Cloth of Gold, to convince Henry VIII of England to become his ally against the emperor Charles V.
After the revolution, this tradition endures, namely under the First Empire, when **emperor Napoleon I** addresses these words during a sumptuous dinner : « Gentlemen, France has been saved by you ! ». Even today, through diplomatic receptions, the art of fine dining contributes to exerting the influence of France over the whole world.

Afterwards, the great turning point in Parisian gastronomy is due to the **French cook Beauvilliers** who, in 1782, opens the first true restaurant in Paris : « La grande taverne de Londres », on the Rue de Richelieu.

This great restaurant, the first of its kind in Paris, is constituted of richly decorated rooms, elegant lounges, a perfect service and mostly an exquisite cuisine as well as an admirable cave. Endowed with an excellent memory, Beauvilliers is capable of recognizing his guests and guiding them in their choices. He had been the Chef of the Count of Provence, hence, he greets his guests with the sword on the lap and

the official uniform (officier de bouche de réserve). He remains for more than twenty years unrivaled for the Parisian upper class. In 1814, he publishes « L'art du cuisinier », where he writes about cooking, the order of dishes and service.

After the success of Beauvilliers, the concept of restaurant largely evolves between 1790 and 1814, when the great cooks from aristocratic houses find themselves out of work after the nobles flee abroad; therefore they decide to open their own restaurants. As such, under the influence of the French Revolution, the Grande Cuisine makes its way to the general public.

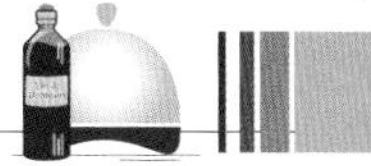

Where taste is concerned, French seasonings such as shallots and spring onions, but also anchovies and, above all, the famous truffle replaced spices as of the XVIIth century. The contrast between savory and sweet remains one of the main characteristics of French taste until the XXth century, after the introduction of sweet in the French cuisine in the XVIth century under the Italian influence. However, it is first and foremost the use of butter, first used in Italy in fine cooking, that becomes the distinctive trait of great French cuisine.

Hence, the France of the Third Republic (1870-1940) is marked by a rich and bourgeois cuisine, consisting of never-ending banquets and menus. This tradition carries on to the seventies, until the emergence of the « nouvelle cuisine », which strives to be natural, dietary and original. This is due to two food critics, Christian Millau and Henri Gault, who call upon chefs to innovate, lighten their sauces, preserve the flavor of the produce and be more receptive to foreign cuisines.

This period is characterized by great chefs who left their marks on the gastronomy of the country and even worldwide for some people : Paul Bocuse, the Troisgros brothers, Alain Chapel, André Pic...

After one generation characterized by excesses, too much innovation that killed innovation, the great French cuisine initiated, towards the end of the eighties, a return to authentic regional produce, without abandoning the lessons in finesse taught by the nouvelle cuisine •

# .3. Festivals and Events all year round

## ALL YEAR ROUND

### Les Plans d'Avril

*Festival of live performance in Paris*

***APRIL***

A team of professionals of show business and communication works for the development of new broadcasting methods close to artists and their projects.

www.plansdavril.com

### fête de la musique

*(Music Festival)*

***JUNE***

Each year, the arrival of summer is celebrated throughout France. Improvised scenes, concerts in bars or in prestigious halls open for the occasion bring happiness to all music-loving of all sorts of people. Thus, everybody is also free to play in front of their door! In Paris, it is a tradition that a huge free concert be given at the Place de la République (Republic Square). Thus, the partying spirit spreads across the entire city : Place de la Nation (Nation Square), Place de la Bastille (Bastille Square), St-Michel Boulevard, on the Champs-Elysées…

www.fetedelamusique.culture.fr

## National Day

If the 14th of July is celebrated all over France, the National day takes on a special significance in Paris. In the morning, a military parade on the Champs Elysées takes place, broadcast on all national chains. In the evening, fireworks are shot mostly from the Champs de Mars, at the base of the Eiffel Tower. Also, during the whole day, tricolor flags and the Marseillaise as a sonorous background. To be equally noted : the firemen ball, in all the caserns of Paris, on the evenings of the 13th and 14th of July; free entry.

## FESTIVAL SOUS LA PLAGE

***JULY–AUGUST***

Electronic music festival taking place some summer Sundays at the André Citroën park :
programming, access plan and log book.

www.souslaplage.com

## ALL YEAR ROUND

### Paris Quartier d'Eté

***The Parisian Summer Festival***

***JULY–AUGUST***

Program, calendar, places and practical information are provided to you. Ten years of dance festival, cinema, or theater are under consultation.

www.quartierdete.com

### festival rock en seine

***AUGUST***

Programming, artists and access plan at the national property of Saint Cloud.

www.rockenseine.com

### Villette numérique

***International Festival of numeric arts***

***SEPTEMBER–OCTOBER***

It gathers actors of international numeric culture and invites you to discover how artists redefine the outlines of contemporary creation.

www.villette-numerique.com

Techno Parade & Rendez-Vous Electroniques

septembre

Le succ?s de la premi?re ?dition de la Techno Parade, qui avait rassembl? 170000 personnes dans les rues de Paris en 1998, en a fait un rendez-vous annuel incontournable pour tous les 'techno?des' de la capitale. Jusqu'en l'an 2000, ce rassemblement a pris la forme d'une parade des chars d?filaient au rythme de la musique techno, tandis qu'une faune d'ann?e en ann?e toujours plus jeune et d?guis?e, investissait la rue. Depuis 2001 plus de parade mais de nombreuses sc?nes qui promettent une ambiance survolt?e. En parall?le se d?roulent les Rendez-Vous Electroniques : conf?rences, expositions et animations sp?ciales dans de nombreux bars mettent cette musique ? l'honneur

www.technopol.net

## *Techno Parade et Rendez-vous Electroniques*

***SEPTEMBRE***

The success of the first edition of the Techno Parade, which gathered 170,000 people in the streets of Paris in 1998, has made it an annual rendezvous not to be missed for all « technoids » of the capital. Up until the year 2000, this gathering has taken the form of a parade : floats marched at the rhythm of techno music, whereas a mob, each year younger and disguised, invaded the street. Since 2001, no more parade but numerous scenes promise a wild ambiance. At the same time, Electronic Rendezvous take place : conferences, exhibitions, and special events in numerous bars celebrate this music.

www.technopol.net

## Festival d'Automne à Paris

*(Paris Autumn Festival)*

***SEPTEMBER TO DECEMBER***

he autumn festival is dedicated to contemporary art. It is aimed at housing reference Art works, unpublished in France : dance, music, cinema, and arts.

www.festival-automne.com

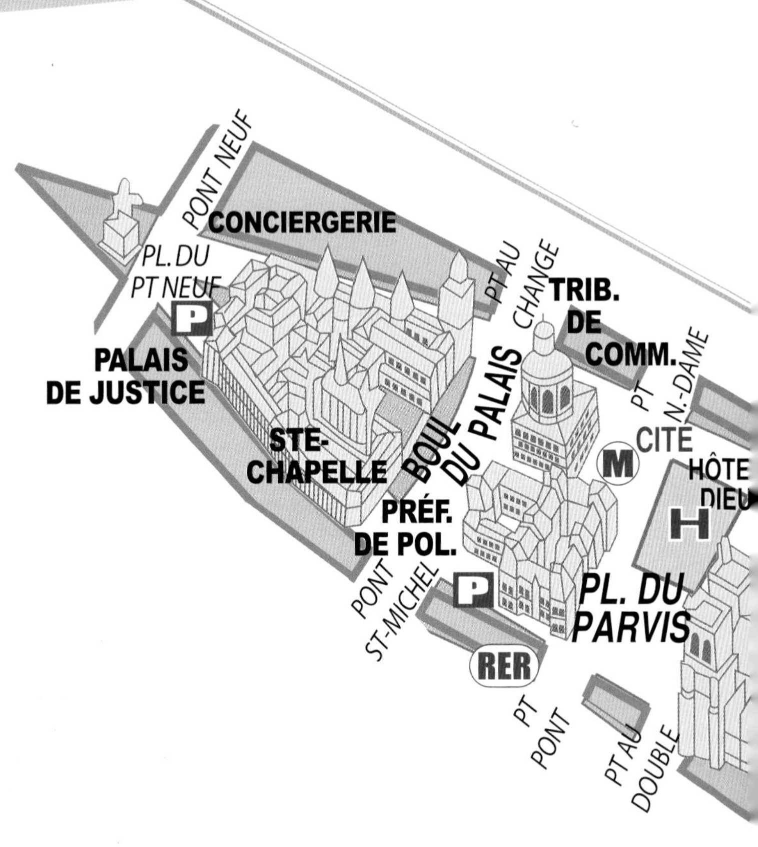
PONT NEUF
CONCIERGERIE
PL. DU
PT NEUF
P
PALAIS
DE JUSTICE
STE-
CHAPELLE
PT AU
CHANGE
TRIB.
DE
COMM.
PT
N.-DAME
BOUL
DU PALAIS
CITÉ
M
HÔTE
DIEU
H
PRÉF.
DE POL.
PONT
ST-MICHEL
P
PL. DU
PARVIS
RER
PT
PONT
PT AU
DOUBLE

# .4.
# Visit itineraries in Paris

## .1st Itinerary.

### The « Île de la Cité », cradle of Paris

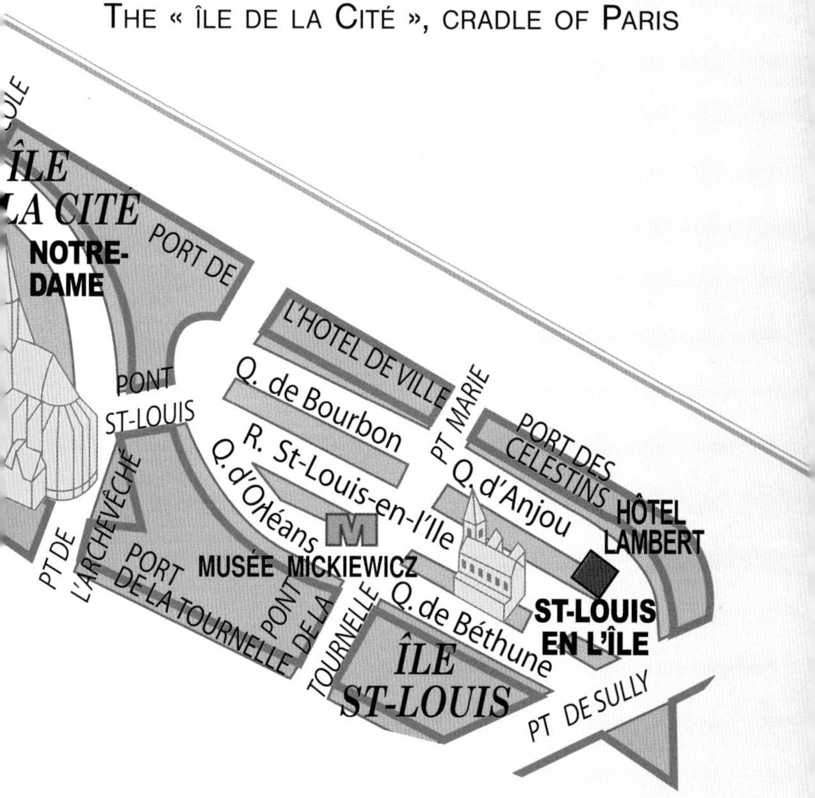

ÎLE
LA CITÉ
NOTRE-DAME
PORT DE
L'HOTEL DE VILLE
PONT ST-LOUIS
Q. de Bourbon
PT MARIE
PORT DES CELESTINS
R. St-Louis-en-l'Ile
Q. d'Orléans
Q. d'Anjou
HÔTEL LAMBERT
PT DE L'ARCHEVÊCHÉ
PORT DE LA TOURNELLE
MUSÉE MICKIEWICZ
PONT DE LA TOURNELLE
Q. de Béthune
ST-LOUIS EN L'ÎLE
ÎLE ST-LOUIS
PT DE SULLY

## THE « ÎLE DE LA CITÉ », CRADLE OF PARIS

**ÎLE DE LA CITÉ** is the historic cradle of Paris city. It shelters the « Parisii » tribe-Celtic word referring to a boat on the water-when the Romans, headed by Labienus, the Cesar's lieutenant, conquer it in 52 BC. Hence, the city bears the roman name of « Lutèce » (Lutetia), from the latin word Lutum, which means mud. During the barbarian invasions, citizens galvanized by Sainte-Genevieve take refuge in the Île de La Cité, which is easier to defend. Clovis, king of the Franks and conqueror of the Romans in 486, adopts it as his capital. Thus, during the Carolingian period, life revolves around the Île de La Cité.

During the IXth century, Norman invasions threaten Paris which is subjected to frequent assaults by Vikings. The latter lay siege to it in 885 and the defense commanded by Count Eudes and the bishop of Paris Gozlin is once more orchestrated around the Île de La Cité.

This location preserves its role as a religious and judicial center all along the Middle Ages. Notre-Dame, the works of which start in 1163 on a sacred site of the roman epoch under the aegis of the Bishop of Paris, Maurice de Sully, along with the Sainte Chapelle, built in 1245 under the reign of St. Louis, and the Conciergerie, is one of the last vestiges of the Middle Ages on the isle. Moreover, one could discover on the square of Notre Dame the layout of roads from that era, shaped as a flagstone that allows setting distances that separate the cities of the province from the capital, a proof of the role of the Île de La Cité as a historic center in the Middle Ages.

The **ILE SAINT-LOUIS** is originally formed by two islets : the « Île aux vaches » (Cows

*>> Notre-Dame de Paris*

isle)-as it was merely a pasture field-and the « île Notre-Dame » where the duels used to take place during the Middle Ages. It is not before the XVIIth century that the two islets are reunified by Christophe Marie, general contractor of the bridges of France, who builds the bridge that still bears his name until the present day. At that time, this is where nobles and bourgeois built their residences, and one can still discover there today splendid private mansions.

This magnificent set, the Île de la Cité and the Île Saint Louis, is related to the rest of Paris city by several splendid bridges which traveled down the ages

>> *Pont Marie*

In 1635, Christophe Marie builds the **PONT MARIE** (Marie bridge) situated on the northern side of the Île Saint Louis which we just evoked, on the foundations of existing houses, in the framework of the urban-planning of Île Notre-Dame under the reign of Louis XIII. It is reshaped in the XIXth century, but still keeps its initial name.

>> *Pont Sully*

The **PONT SULLY** (Sully Bridge) is situated at the eastern tip of the Île Saint Louis. The first two footbridges that initially form it date back to 1838. They were then suspended and pedestrian.
The footbridge on the left bank bears the name « Constantine », and the one on the right bank is named « Damiette ».

The 1870 war prevents their replacement by a fixed bridge planned for under the Second Empire. It is not before March 1876 that a new cast iron bridge, designed by engineers Vaudrey and Brosselin is installed.

Also on the Île Saint Louis, but more to the south, Louis XIII, aged 13, and his mother queen Marie of Medicis lay the first stone of the **PONT DE LA TOURNELLE** (Tournelle Bridge) on October 11, 1614, replacing the old bridge that dates back to 1369. The contractor Christophe Marie, who is also in charge of building the housing of the Île Saint-Louis as well as two other bridges in the ten following years, starts its construction in 1618. It is finished in 1620 and is made of wood, same as the preceding bridget.

*>> Pont de La Tournelle*

The bridge is swept along by ice in 1637 then reconstructed. Because of the 1651 floods, it is severely damaged and the architect Noblet decides to rebuild it in stone between 1654 and 1656. In 1658, it is once again greatly damaged by ice, but it won't be replaced by the present bridge until 1928.

The **PONT LOUIS PHILIPPE** (Louis Philippe Bridge), at the western tip of the isle, on the left bank side, is open to traffic on July 26, 1834 by King Louis Philippe, who lays the first stone on July 29, 1833.
During the 1848 revolution, a fire destroys a part of the bridge joining Île Saint-Louis to the left bank. The suspension cables of the upstream part melt, rushing about twenty victims to water. All tollbooths are also set on fire.

>> *Pont Louis Philippe*

Following these events, it is renamed Pont de la Réforme (Reform Bridge). After the toll is removed, the traffic intensifies so much that it becomes necessary to limit the crossing. The 1860 decree orders its replacement only on the right bank side of the Seine, and plans for a construction made of stone, resting on two piles of 4 meters width, with pillars cast by a bottomless caisson made of concrete. The main arch measures 32 meters while the lateral ones are of 30 meters. Bull's eyes light up the galleries containing gas and water pipes. Its extension on the left bank side shall not be reconstructed.

The President of Paris Council and the Prefect of the Seine inaugurated the **PONT SAINT LOUIS** (Saint Louis Bridge), which links the two isles, on 28 Oct 1970. This bridge is most of all functional, with no particular esthetic design; it constitutes in fact no obstacle for navigation.

The roadway rests on two caissons girders of 200 tons each; the abutments are based on anchored wells foundations, standing and plated against the masonry of the quay walls. It totally clears the waterway.

When coming back from the Place du Parvis, one discovers the majestic **CATHÉDRALE NOTRE-DAME** (Notre-Dame Cathedral), which dominates this square.

The construction of the present gothic cathedral, fruit of the ambition of Bishop Maurice de Sully, starts around 1160. The whole building is completed as of the XIIth century. Some modifications are carried out in the subsequent century, following the architectural canons of the « glowing » gothic style, very fashionable at the time.

Around 1250, Jean de Chelles completes the northern arm and starts building the southern arm, which shall be completed by Jean de Montreuil. From the middle of the XIIIth century until the early XIVth century, chapels are built amongst the buttresses of the nave. Pierre de Montreuil is the designer of the ones leaning on the chevet.

The gothic cathedral is largely modified later on due to restorations carried out in the XIIIth century as well as revolutionary destructions. Restoration works, to which the cathedral owes its current shape, are completed in 1864 and are carried out by Jean-Baptiste Lassus and mainly by Viollet-le-Duc. They are aimed at restituting the XIIth century architecture and equally include sculptures, furniture, stained-glass windows... Each of these aspects contributes today to the prestige of Notre-Dame de Paris.

>> Notre-Dame de Paris

The original southern portal of the western façade, dedicated to the Virgin, is deemed among the masterpieces of gothic sculpture. Some old masters painted namely by Le Brun and Jouvenet, have been replaced in the chapels by « Mays », commissioned by the fraternity of silversmiths from 1630 to 1707 and offered every 1st of May, which explains their designation.

At the eastern tip of the île de la Cité, right behind the Cathedral, stands the Pont de l'Archevêché (Archbishopric Bridge). It bears the name of the old archbishopric, which buildings disappeared after the revolution of 1789. This bridge is built in 1828 according to the plans of contractor Plouard. It is a toll bridge, same as many other bridges of that epoch. Thus, it costs one penny per pedestrian and two pennies per horse. In 1848, the city buys back this right, initially foreseen until 1876.

The **Pont au Double** (Double Bridge), left bank side, originates from the enlargement of Hôtel-Dieu hospital particularly overcrowded at that epoch due to numerous epidemics that hit the capital. In 1515, the only available building area is the small arm of the Seine River, situated at the left bank. The city opposes it fearing it might obstruct navigation.

>> Pont au Double

Therefore, it is only in 1626 that the building authorization is granted, but at the hospital's expenses. This agreement

provides for the construction of the bridge on 3 arches during a period of six years; followed by the buildings two years later. However, as of 1627, under popular pressure, the state addresses a formal notice to the administrators to allow the passage of riverside residents. A toll system is applied with double the price, which explains the name of the bridge.

>> *The view from the Pont d'Arcole*

The insalubrity of hospital rooms, the pouring out of garbage, the wash houses under the piles, the density of buildings that do not allow the air nor the sun in, compel the city to resort to the bridge's destruction in 1847. Hence, it is replaced by a unique arch of masonry. In 1883, it is demolished once again and replaced by a metallic arch, which still exists until our present day.

On the opposite side of the isle, the Pont d'Arcole (Arcole Bridge) is one of the most ancient iron bridges built in France. Constructed in 1854-1855 by engineer Oudry, it is formed by a unique arch lowered by 90 meters.

The **PETIT-PONT** (Small-Bridge), on the right bank side, facing the square of Notre-Dame

>> *Pont Notre-Dame*

Cathedral, bears this name since twenty centuries.

Lutetia is not yet occupied by the Romans when a footbridge links the small island of Lutetia to the left bank. Built in stone in 1186 due to the generosity of the Archbishop of Paris Maurice de Sully, it is today in the same state it was in 1853.

The **PONT NOTRE-DAME** (Notre-Dame Bridge) is situated on the right bank. It was originally made of wood and named Notre-Dame. Moreover, Charles VI set up its first pile in 1413.

The bridge, which reconstruction is planned for 1440 thanks to a tax levied on the returns of mill boats, collapses on October 25, 1499 because the works were never carried out. A dozen corrupt civil servants are arrested and end up their lives in prison, having failed to pay the heavy penalties.

It is rebuilt in stone from 1501 to 1512 with 34 houses labeled with golden numbers, even from one side, and odd from the other which is considered as unique and futuristic at that epoch. This bridge shall become the triumphal path for kings François I, Henri II, Charles IX, Henri III, Louis XIV, and the Infant of Spain. Moreover, Notre-Dame Bridge is considered as the most fashionable and the most festive bridge. Houses are torn down in 1787 and the bridge becomes suitable for vehicles. It is reconstructed in 1853 then in 1913.

On the western part of the 'île de la Cité, the **CONCIERGERIE** and the **SAINTE-CHAPELLE,** are considered as the vestiges of the most ancient Parisian royal palace, the Palais de la Cité (City Palace) transformed into a prison in the XVth century.

On the location that used to be the residence of Roman Governors and later that of the first Capetians, Philippe le Bel builds, in the early XIVth century, a palace representing his power, described then as the most sumptuous palace of the Middle Ages.

Towards the end of the XIVth century, Capetian kings abandon the Palais de la Cité (City Palace) to reside at the Louvre and Vincennes, conceding the place for the Parisian Parliament and the kingdom's central

>> *Palais de la Cité*

administrations. The Concierge, origin of the word « Conciergerie », nominated by the king to establish and keep the order, as well as to record the names of prisoners, is behind transforming part of the building into a prison.

In the rooms that used to serve as a Terror area during the French Revolution and which can be visited today, the cell of Marie-Antoinette and a series of dungeons are restored. The chapel called « des Girondins » (the Girondists), the expiatory chapel designed according to Louis XVIII's wishes on the same location of Marie-Antoinette's cell, in addition to the women courtyard and the « salle de la toilette », constitute touching witnesses of the revolutionary epoch.

On the left bank side, in the continuation of the Palace Boulevard, stands the **Pont Saint-Michel** (Saint-Michel Bridge). Erected in stone from 1378 to 1387 by Hugues Aubriot, it is successively called « Petit-pont », « Petit-pont-Neuf », and « Pont-Neuf ». It is carried away by ice towards the

>> The «N» of Napoleon on the Pont au Change

end of January 1408 along with the houses it included. Rebuilt eight years later, it is baptized in 1424 in the name of the neighboring church, Saint-Michel.

On December 9, 1547, it is hit by a boat and collapses with the seventeen houses that are constructed therein. Rebuilt in wood in 1549, it is later on swept along by the flood of 1616. Reconstructed in stone, it holds thirty two houses from each side until 1786, and then their demolition is carried out. The last houses shall not be pulled down until 1809. The bridge is entirely rebuilt by Vaudrey in 1857.

On the other side of the Seine River, the **Pont au Change** (Exchange Bridge) is built in 1859 by the engineers La Gallisserie & Vaudrey. It comprises three elliptic arches in masonry. Its design is composed of an «N» -Napoleon's initial- in a crown of laurels, which meets that of Saint-Michel Bridge.

The **Pont-Neuf** (New Bridge) is the most renowned bridge in Paris. It is situated at the western tip of the Île de Cité. Henri III laid down the first stone on May 31st, 1578. Accomplished only in 1604, it is already distinguished by being the first houseless bridge. It stretches out on 238 meters length and 20

>> Pont-Neuf

meters width, and is divided into two uneven parts, with seven arches on the great arm, right bank side, and five arches on the small arm, left bank side. This bridge is designed by Androuet Du Cerceau and stands out as well by its architecture : the famous half-moon turrets, and most of all, the famous grotesque masks or « mascarons », which number totals 384, arranged on the consoles supporting the cornices

GALERIE NATIONALE
DU JEU DE PAUME
MUSÉE DE
L'ORANGERIE
TUILERIES
JARDIN
DES
TUILERIES
MUSÉE DE LA MODE
DU TEXTILE ET DES
ARTS DECORATIFS
QUAI
DES
TUILERIES
PASSERELLE DE SOLFERINO
PONT ROYAL
PORT DU

## •2nd Itinerary•

# THE LOUVRE AND THE PALAIS ROYAL (ROYAL PALACE)

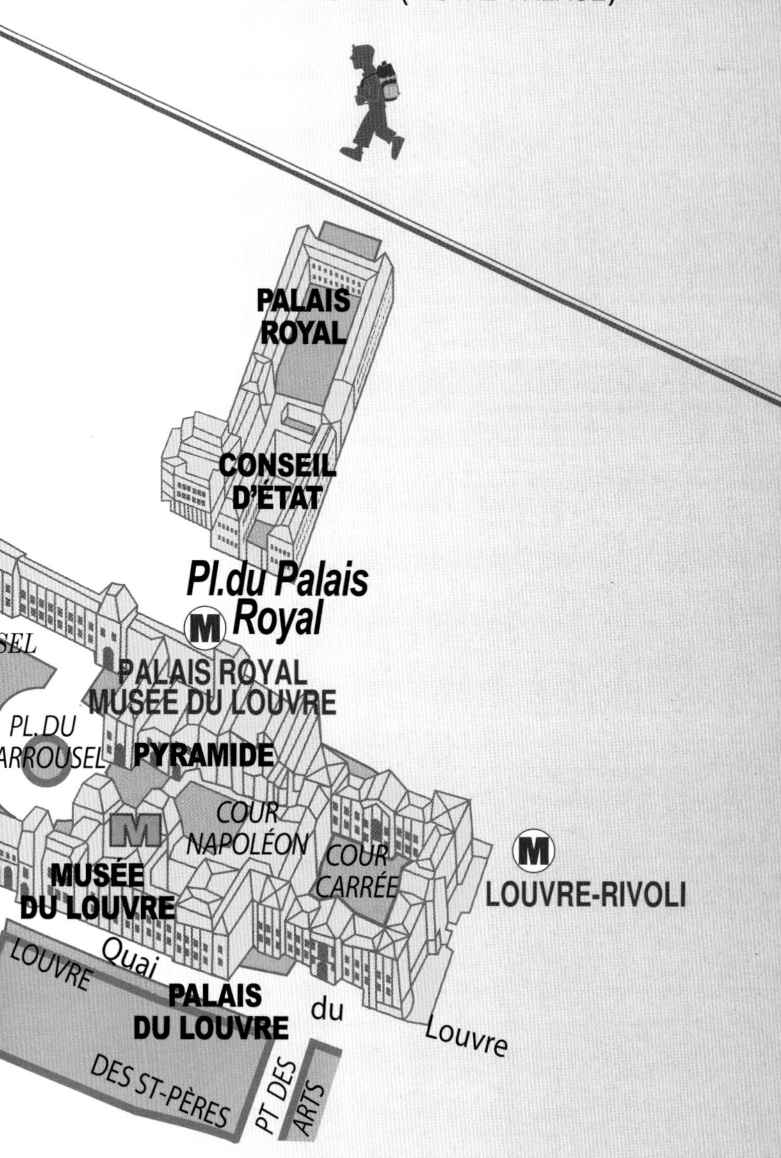

THE LOUVRE AND
THE PALAIS ROYAL (ROYAL PALACE)

# The Louvre

## >> ACCESS

*By metro (subway) :*
Palais-Royal station / Louvre museum.

*By bus :*
Bus n° 21,24,27,39,48,68,69,72,81,95
The Paris Open Tour : stop facing the pyramid.

*By car :*
Un parc de stationnement souterrain est accessible par l'avenue du général Lemonier, tous les jours de 7h00 à 23h00.

*By Batobus (bus boat) :*
Stop over at the Louvre, François Mitterrand quay.

*From Orly airport :*
RER C in the direction of Champs de Mars-Tour Eiffel, get off at Saint-Michel Notre-Dame, walk until Saint Michel, take the bus no. 27 heading towards Saint Lazare, get off at Musée du Louvre, facing the Pyramid.

*From Charles de Gaulle airport :*
RER B in the direction of Massy-Palaiseau, change at Châtelet les Halles, take the line 14 towards saint-Lazare, get off at the Pyramids and walk until the Louvre museum or take the line 1 and get off at Palais-Royal/Louvre museum.

## >> THE LOUVRE HISTORY

Its origin dates back to 1200, when Philippe Auguste, already settled at the Île de la Cité, erects a fortress next to the Seine River as well as a dungeon protecting this new fence. This fortress is located southwest of the present Cour Carrée and one can still discover today vestiges in the archeological crypt of the museum.

In 1358, following the insurrection of Etienne Marcel, Charles V decides to turn the Louvre into a royal residence while maintaining its military defenses. His successors shall prefer the Hotel St. Paul and the Hotel des Tournelles to the Louvre.

As to François I, he orders the razing of the dungeon and entrusts Pierre Lescot with the task of turning the Louvre into a Renaissance Palace. However, works are not finished when François I dies in 1547. The western and southern wings are erected under the reign of Henri II. Catherine of Médicis decides, after the death of Henri II, to take up residence in the Louvre and to link the Palace to the Tuileries, which she intends to develop as an Italian-style park. Works will only start in 1594 under the reign of Henri IV who commissions the construction of the Grande Galerie (Big Gallery) as a supplement to the Petite Galerie (Small Gallery).

*>> The Louvre*

In 1659, Louis XIII decides to build the Pavillon de l'Horloge (Clock Pavilion) and entrusts architects Lemercier and LeVau with the project. Thus the pavilion is extended with a main body of buildings. Later on, Louis XIV decides to enlarge the Louvre and entrusts Levau with the task of quadrupling the area of the Cour Carrée. As to the Tuileries Garden, it is expanded by Le Nôtre. Despite the works already achieved, Louis XIV settles in the Versailles Palace.

It is only after the revolutionary turmoil that Bonaparte gives the order to enlarge the Place du Carrousel where he erects the Arc de Triomphe (Triumph Arch) as a tribute to his conquests. He also decides to build the wing that runs alongside Rivoli Street; nevertheless works interrupted under the Restoration shall only be re-launched under the Second Empire, with the help of Visconti.

>> *A statue in the Jardin des Tuileries*

During the 1871 Commune, the Tuileries are set on fire. Hence, in 1882 architect Lefuel is assigned to reconstruct the Flore & Marsan pavilions. Nowadays, the Louvre has been subject to multiple improvements, such as the Leoh Ming Pei Pyramid, in order to become the greatest museum of the world.

## >> THE MUSEUM

*Opening hours of the museum :*

The museum is open every day of the week except on Tuesdays and some public holidays, from 9:00am until 18:00pm. By night, it is open until 21:45pm on Wednesdays and Fridays.

Access by the pyramid and by the Carrousel Gallery is open from 9:00am till 22:00pm except on Tuesdays.

The Richelieu passage is open from 9:00am to 18:00pm, except on Tuesdays. The entrance via the « Porte des Lions » is accessible from 9:00am to 17:30pm, except on Tuesdays and Fridays.

*Access to the museum :*

> ***Tickets are available on the same day*** for the Louvre museum, except for the exhibitions of the Napoleon hall and the Eugène-Delacroix museum.

> ***Tickets are available for the night shifts*** at the Louvre on Wednesday and Friday, except for the exhibitions of the Napoleon Hall.

> ***Free for all;***
The first Sunday of the month and on July 14th.

> ***Free for youth aged less than 26 years;***
Entrance to the museum is free of charge for young people aged less than 26 years on Friday nights from 18:00 to 21:45, except for the exhibitions of the Napoleon Hall.

> ***All year long, free access to the Louvre museum and to the Eugène-Delacroix museum*** is granted, on presentation of a valid written proof, for :
-Young people under 18 years old;
-Job seekers and beneficiaries of social minimums (written proof less than 6 months old);
-Handicapped visitors and their accompanying people;
-Active teachers of arts history, art history, fine arts, decorative arts, on presentation of written proofs mentioning the course they teach;
-Plastic artists affiliated to the Maison des Artistes (House of Artists) and to the International association of fine arts, the AIAP (Association Internationale des Arts Plastiques).

The Louvre museum, old residence of the kings of France, has been for two centuries the greatest museum of the world. The Louvre museum exhibits works of occidental art from the Middle Ages until 1848, of antique civilizations that preceded and influenced it as well as Islamic arts. Its collections are divided into eight departments with their respective history, linked to curators, to collectors, and to donors :

## Oriental Antiquities

The Oriental Antiquities department of the Louvre museum is dedicated to ancient civilizations of the Near and Middle East countries, over a period that extends from the birth of villages that appeared over 10,000 years ago until the coming of Islam.

## Egyptian Antiquities

The Egyptian antiquities department displays vestiges of successive civilizations of the Nile borders, from the end of Prehistory (around 4000 years prior to our era) until the Christian epoch (as of the IVth century AD).

## Greek, Etruscan, and Roman Antiquities

This department gathers artworks from three civilizations : Greek, Etruscan and Roman, which illustrate the artistic activity of a vast region : Greece, Italy and the whole Mediterranean region, the history of which stretches out from the Neolithic epoch (IVth millenary BC) to the VIth century of our present era..

## Paintings

The paintings department complies with the encyclopedic dimension of the museum with artworks that represent all European painting schools, from the XIIIth century to 1848. The study and setting-off of the collections are entrusted to twelve curators that are amongst the greatest specialists.

## Sculptures

Fitted out as of 1824, the « modern » sculpture halls become progressively a department for medieval, Renaissance and modern sculptures, after being separated from antiquities collections (1848) then from arts objects (1893).

## Art Objects

The department of art objects presents a world of objects from various shapes, materials, and epochs; from jewelry to tapestries, as well as ivory, bronze, ceramics and furniture. One could find artworks from the Middle Ages to the first half of the XIXth century.

## Islamic Arts

The Islamic arts department displays thousands of artworks mainly destined to the court or to fortunate elite. Born of one thousand and three hundred years of history and from three continents, they are the witnesses of diversity in inspiration and creativity of Islamic lands.

## Graphic Arts (Prints and drawings)

Works on paper using all techniques constitute the collection of one of the eight departments that form the museum. Due to their fragility when exposed to light, they are temporarily exhibited and a consultation hall allows the public to have access to each artwork upon a previous request.

In the continuation of the Cour Carré, the **PONT DES ARTS** (Arts Bridge) is constructed between 1802 and 1804 by engineers Louis-Alexandre de Cessart and Jacques Dillon. It is the first metalwork of such caliber ever to be achieved in France.

*>> Pont des Arts*

Light arches of cast iron support a horizontal platform that constitutes an esplanade reserved for pedestrians. Destroyed in 1981, the Pont des Arts is replaced by a copy of steel presenting enlarged arches to allow the crossing of barges. The bridge features numerous arts exhibitions throughout the year.

When leaving the place du Carrousel, towards the Seine river, one finds the **PONT DU CARROUSEL** (Carrousel Bridge), inaugurated on October 30, 1834 by Louis-Philippe. This bridge is open to circulation in 1835; hence toll offices are located in the four pedestals at each entrance of the bridge, but the four statues : L'Abondance, L'Industrie, La Seine,

*>> Pont du Carroussel*

& la Ville de Paris (the Abundance, the Industry, the Seine, and Paris City) of Louis-Messidor Petitot will only be installed in 1846.

## The Palais Royal

When crossing the rue de Rivoli, one finds the **PALAIS ROYAL** (Royal Palace), the construction of which is decided in 1632 by Cardinal Richelieu, who becomes at that time the minister of King Louis XIII. Richelieu commissions the works of the future « Palais Cardinal » (Cardinal Palace) to his favorite architect, Le Mercier, who shall finish it in 1639. The Cardinal dies therein on December 4, 1642. Thus, the palace is bequeathed to the king who also dies the following year.

Anne of Austria and the dauphin, future Louis XIV settle in the palace, which shall henceforth bear the name of « Palais Royal ». Afterwards, the palace is bequeathed to Philippe d'Orléans, brother of Louis XIV and husband of Henriette of England who also dies in the same palace. Philippe II d'Orléans, the Regent, settles later in the palace where several libertine suppers are organized. His great grandson, Philippe Egalité commands the construction of buildings that house boutiques all around the gardens. He also has the French Theatre built.

During the Revolution, the « Palais Royal » is in the heart of events and becomes later a very active center of debauchery mixing gambling houses and sleazy hotels. As of 1801, the « Palais Royal » becomes the seat of the Court, and later the seat of the Bourse (Stock Exchange) and the Commercial Court. In 1814, it is returned to the Orléans family. In 1871, during the events of La Commune, the « Palais Royal » is set on fire. It shall be restored to host the Seat of the « Conseil d'Etat » (Council of State) from 1875 up until now.

On the way back from the Louvre, one enters the **JARDINS DES TUILERIES** (Tuileries Gardens) which go along the Rue de Rivoli, towards the Place de la Concorde.

*>> The Arc de Triomphe of Carroussel*

Their origin goes back to 1553, when Catherine of Medicis decides to settle in the Louvre and to build a Castle therein. She buys pieces of land in the Tuileries and builds an Italian style park with fountains, a grotto, a greenhouse as well as a menagerie. The Tuileries Gardens rapidly become a popular leisure walk in the XVIth century.

In the XVIIth century, Colbert entrusts Le Nôtre with the works of embellishing the gardens, the plans of which are still preserved to the present day.

At the beginning of the gardens, one notices the **PONT ROYAL** (Royal Bridge) in the direction of the Seine River. It is one of the oldest bridges of Paris. Designed by Jules Hardouin-Mansart and carried out in 1685 by Gabriel, its design in masonry composed of basket-handle arches, underlined by a spun cornice, was innovative for that epoch.

>> Pont Royal

In the direction of the Concorde, the **PASSERELLE DE SOLFÉRINO**, (Solferino footbridge) is striking with the modernity of its architecture. It is in fact very recent, since it is inaugurated in 1999. It is reserved for pedestrians only.
The Solferino footbridge is designed by the architect and engineer Marc Mimram, winner of the international architecture competition launched for this occasion. It comprises only one metal arch of 106 meter of loading, built on the road axis of rue de Castiglione (Ist arrondissement) and rue de Solférino (VIIth arrondissement), allowing to link the Musée d'Orsay to the Tuileries Garden in replacement of the old bridge dating from the XIXth century

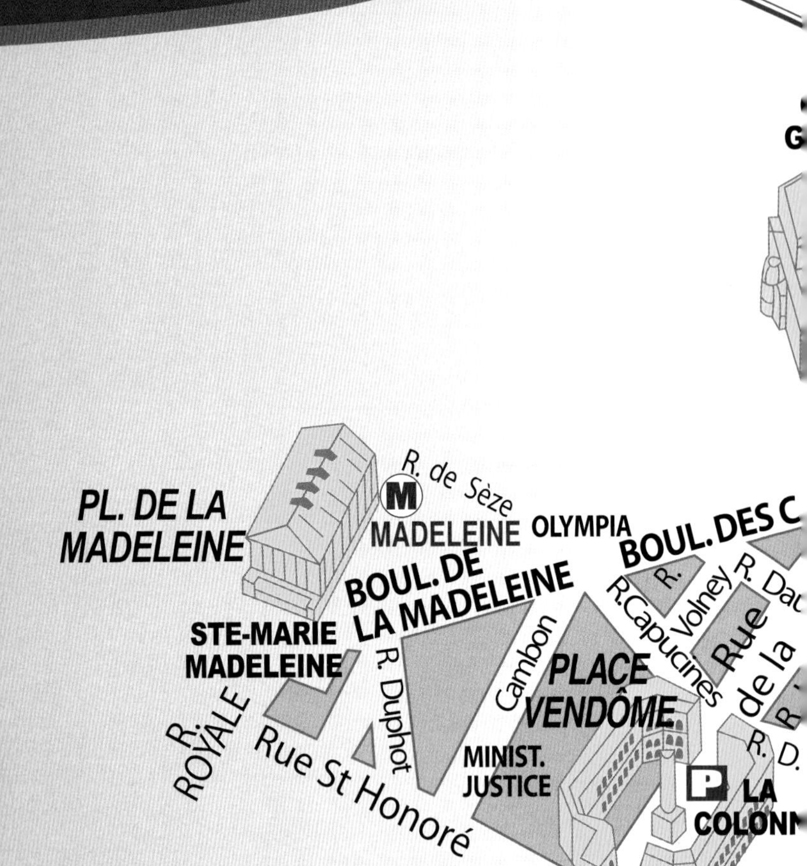
PL. DE LA
MADELEINE
R. de Sèze
MADELEINE
OLYMPIA
BOUL. DES C
BOUL. DE
LA MADELEINE
R.
R.Capucines
Volney
R. Dau
Rue
de la
STE-MARIE
MADELEINE
R. Duphot
Cambon
PLACE
VENDÔME
R.
ROYALE
Rue St Honoré
MINIST.
JUSTICE
R. D.
LA
COLONN

•3rd Itinerary•

## Stylish Paris, Prestigious Paris

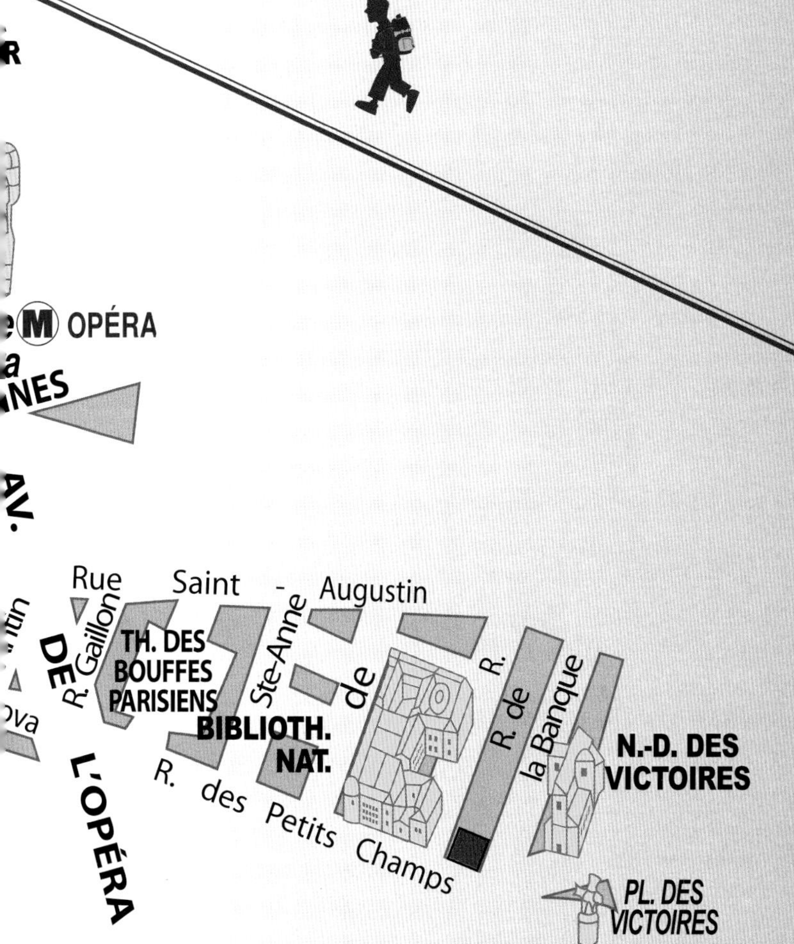

LVDOVICO

## STYLISH PARIS, PRESTIGIOUS PARIS

When coming out of the Palais Royal, one discovers at the end of the rue des Petits Champs, the magnificent **PLACE DES VICTOIRES** (Victory square).

This square with its circular shape is designed in 1685 to serve as a frame for the allegorical statue of Louis XIV. The duke of La Feuillade assigns Desjardins to undertake the construction works. Destroyed during the Revolution, the statue is replaced by another bronze one achieved by the sculptor Bosio.

The Place des Victoires is considered, since many generations, a fashion hot spot. During the XIXth century, it used to attract young women who dreamt of cashmere they would wear once they are allowed to by their future spouse status. Shawls were part of the groom's wedding presents, same as jewels and laces. The majority of the trendiest shawl makers of the period settled at the square, in the current rue Etienne-Marcel as well as in neighboring streets.

The emergence of a new generation of fashion designers, who were settled at first in neighboring galleries, rejuvenated the square : Kenzo, the precursor, shall leave his first boutique under the arcades of Vivienne crossing, a hundred meters away, and settle in the Place des Victoires, where he establishes his leading boutique. His current neighbors are Thierry Muggler, Cacharel, Esprit, Blanc Bleu, and very recently Van Dutch. For lack of space, the Etienne Marcel street hosts new creators such as Anne Fontaine, Joseph, etc.

Also in the 1st arrondissement, the **PLACE VENDÔME** (Vendôme square) is the square of luxury par excellence. In the continuation of the prestigious rue de la Paix, this square houses the most famous French Jewelers : Cartier, Boucheron, Chaumet, Chopard…, as well as one Paris' most beautiful palaces : the Ritz hotel.

First baptized « Place des Conquêtes » (Conquests Square), then Place Louis-Le-Grand, and Place des Piques (Pikes square) during the Revolution, the « Place Vendôme » owes its name to the Vendôme Hotel which was destroyed in 1687 in order to build the square in its place.

*>> On the right, Colonne Vendôme*
*>> Below, the fresco of the Colonne*

>> Place Vendôme

The Place Vendôme originally framed the equestrian statue of Louis XIV designed by Girardon. Boffard and Hardouin-Mansart, the architects in charge of carrying out the works, erected the first façades on three sides, leaving the southern side open. Only a few years later, it was designed in its octagonal final shape.

The works engaged to build the Vendôme column shall not start before the First Empire. With 43.50 meters of height, it is intended to replace a statue of Liberty erected during the Revolution. First dubbed as the Austerlitz Column, it represents the main feats of arms in the Napoleonic campaigns between 1805 and 1807. Originally surmounted by a Gaudhet statue representing Napoleon I as Julius Caesar, this appendage undergoes many modifications with the change of regimes. Hence, in 1814, during the « One hundred days » war, royalists replace it by a statue of Henri IV. As to Louis-Philippe, he erects a colossal fleur-de-lys. During the Restoration phase, Louis XVIII refurbishes a statue of Napoleon in military uniform.

The column is torn down in 1871, during the « Commune », before being re-erected in the period of the IIIrd Republic with a replica of the original statue of Napoleon as Caesar. Today, the square is considered as a hot spot for luxurious Parisian activities.

When going up the rue de la Paix, the **PALAIS DE L'OPÉRA GARNIER** (Opéra Garnier Palace) greets strollers. A true masterpiece of theatre architecture of the XIXth century, the « Palais Garnier », built by Charles Garnier and inaugurated in 1875, is the thirteenth opera house in Paris since the creation of this institution by Louis XIV in 1669.

Its construction was initiated by Napoleon III among other important renovation projects in the capital, successfully conducted under his reign by Baron Haussmann. This historical monument is open to visitors who can namely admire the famous ceiling of the Opera Room by Chagall. The Opéra Garnier also features remarkable Lyrical and choreographic performances.

On the way out of the Opéra, one discovers the **PLACE DE LA MADELEINE** (La Madeleine Square) in the continuation of the Capucines Boulevard.

The neo-classical church of Sainte Marie-Madeleine is built in the style of Greek temples. Works are completed in 1842, after almost one century of modifications and delays. The original plans were inspired from the Church of Saint Louis des Invalides, however, a new architect named Couture, decides to raze the building in order to erect a new edifice directly inspired from the Pantheon.

The works are interrupted between 1790 and 1806, while many projects are developed, amongst which that of Napoleon I who decides to erect, in the same place, a temple for the glory of the Grande Armée. He commissions Vignon for that mission, thus the building is razed one more time.

In 1814, Louis XVIII confirms the vocation of La Madeleine as a church. However, in 1837, the building is almost transformed into a railway station that hosts the first railway line linking Paris to Saint-Germain. Nevertheless, La Madeleine is consecrated as a church in 1842.

The La Madeleine Church is constituted of fifty two pillars of twenty meters height. Its monumental stairway offers one of the most beautiful views of Paris, along the Rue Royale through the Place de la Concorde, the Seine River until the National Assembly. One finds around the Place de la Madeleine the most renowned names of fine and luxurious grocery boutiques such as Fauchon and Hédiard

DES

CHAMPS

M
FRANKILN-
D. ROOSEVELT

## •4th Itinerary•

# The Place de la Concorde (the Concorde Square) and the Champs-Élysées

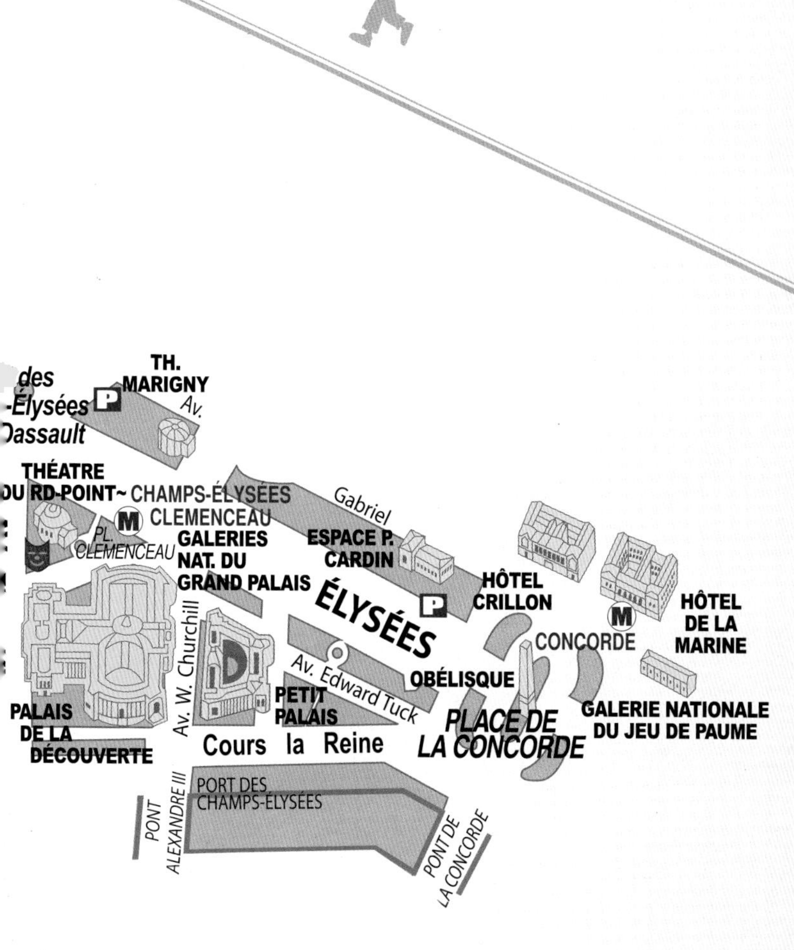

# 4th Itinerary

## The place de la Concorde (Concorde Square) and the Champs Elysées

In the angle of la Madeleine church, the Place de la Concorde (Concorde Square) appears to the visitor. It is undoubtedly the most beautiful square in Paris. With a surface area of 84,000 square meters, it offers an amazing view of the Champs Elysées in their full length from the Jardin des Tuileries (Tuileries Garden) to the Arc de Triomphe (Triumph Arch).

It is erected between 1755 and 1775 by architect Ange-Jacques Gabriel, who wins the architecture competition by presenting a project based on an octagon delimited by a ditch with balustrades surrounding it.

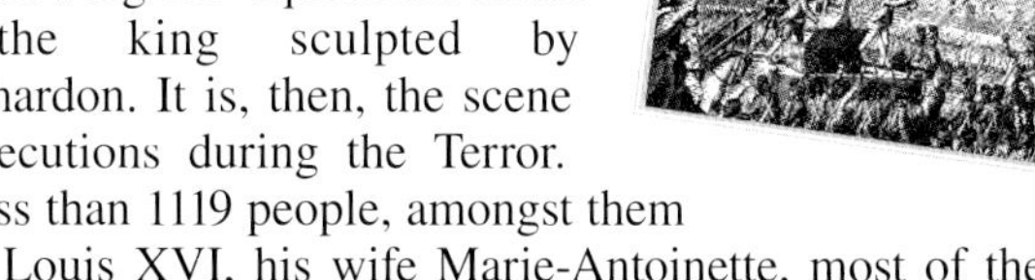

The **Place de la Concorde** originally bore the name of Louis XV, however, it becomes the Revolution square in 1792, after overthrowing the equestrian statue of the king sculpted by Bouchardon. It is, then, the scene of executions during the Terror. No less than 1119 people, amongst them King Louis XVI, his wife Marie-Antoinette, most of their close relatives, as well as the Revolution leaders are guillotined.

After this trouble period, eight statues representing eight different French cities are requested to ornament the pedestals erected around the square. Cortot sculpts Brest and Rouen, Pradier Lille and Strasbourg, Petitot Lyon and Marseille, Caillouette Bordeaux and Nantes. Two fountains, inspired by that of Saint-Peter of Rome, are constructed between 1835 and 1840 at the center of the square. The one at the north represents river navigation and the one on the south maritime navigation.

>> The frescos of the Obelisks, Place de la Concorde
>> On the right, the Obelisk
>> Below, the Pont de la Concorde

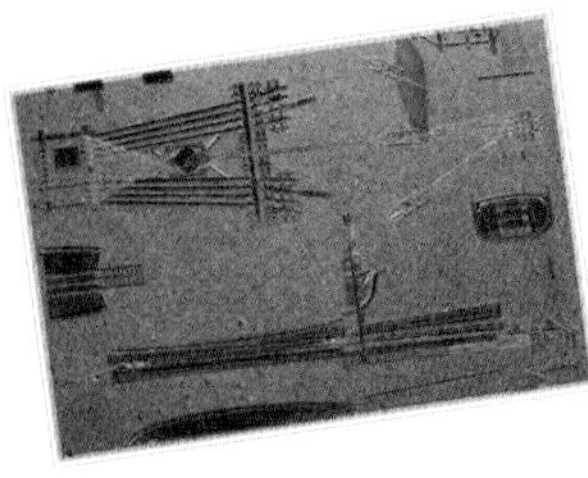

One also notices two twin buildings with colonnades built on one side of the square by Ange-Jacques Gabriel. These buildings delimit the northern side of the square, the Hotel de la Marine which houses the Headquarters of the French Marine, and the Hotel de Crillon, one of the most luxurious hotels in Paris. This is where the Treaty of friendship and exchange between France and the 13 independent American States is signed in February 6, 1778. Benjamin Franklin shall be among the signatories representing the United States. A plate standing against the Rue Royale, commemorates in English and French this Treaty according to which France recognizes the Independence of the United States.

Today, in the exact place where King Louis XVI was guillotined, stands an Obelisk made of pink granite offered to France in 1831 by Muhammad Ali, Vice-King and Pacha of Egypt. This monument which is 3300 years old, weighs tons, and measures 23 meters high, was originally placed at the Thebes Temple (Luxor). It shall be brought to Paris under the reign of Louis-Philippe, after a four year journey. The obelisk is engraved by hieroglyphs. The base describes the technical means having allowed its transportation as well as its erection on the square.

Not very far, the **Pont de la Concorde** (Concorde Bridge) strides over the Seine River. The legend decrees that some of the stones having served for the construction of this bridge come from the destruction of the Bastille. This five-arch-bridge was designed by Jean Rodolphe Perronet, built between 1786 and 1791, and enlarged in 1931. The view it offers overlooking the Palais-Bourbon and the Concorde is remarkable.

When crossing the place de la Concorde, one steps into the **CHAMPS-ÉLYSÉES** avenue, which stretches over almost 2 kilometers of length and is 71 meters large.

Known as « the most beautiful avenue in the world », this large street offers numerous luxury boutiques, prestigious restaurants; it also includes the headquarters of local and international companies adjacent to movie theatres, department stores and fast food businesses that emerged recently.

*>> At the top, a detail of a column, Place de la Concorde*
*>> Below, the avenue of the Champs-Élysées by night*

This avenue, dominated by the Arc de Triomphe, became the symbol of the French armies' glory; in fact, this is where the military parade of July 14th takes place every year.

The architect André Le Nôtre designed the Champs-Elysées avenue in 1670. First named « Grand-cours » then Champs-Elysées, the axis starting from the Tuileries Garden is prolonged until the top of mount Maillot in 1710, then until the gateway bearing the same name, in 1774. The obscure avenue was seldom visited then.

It only started attracting Parisians starting 1779, with its numerous restaurateurs, lemonade makers as well as its palm and ball games. It is probably during the Second Empire that the artery reached the peak of its splendor, since noble families such as the Pereire, the Rothschild and relatives of the Emperor Napoleon III settled there.

>> *The Avenue des Champs-Elysées*

In the XXth century, the avenue was progressively transformed into a residential quarter housing several luxurious businesses (Vuitton, Guerlain, Cartier, etc.) as well as car dealers. The first shopping malls were built after the Great War while the number of movie theaters rapidly increased. However, after World War Two, some luxury businesses moved to other avenues of the quarter, making room namely for airline companies.

In 1994, the City of Paris remodeled the particular appearance of this axis by deciding to clear service roads which are from then on reserved for pedestrians, and by planting new trees, etc.

At the beginning of the Champs Elysées Avenue, the famous **MARLY HORSES** of Guillaume Coustou watch over the entrance of the Place de la Concorde (Concorde Square) since 1795. In fact, these are only replicas that visitors can admire today. Initially designed for the watering place of the Château de Marly (Marly Castle), the authentic horses are preserved from erosion after having been touched up and sheltered at the Louvre in 1984.

One discovers then, on the right side, the famous Ledoyen restaurant which was originally an open-air café named Le Dauphin rented since 1791 by Antoine Nicolas Doyen. The present edifice dates back to 1848 and was erected by Hittorff while redesigning the Champs-Elysées gardens. This prestigious establishment offers two menus : high quality gastronomy on the first floor, simple and more affordable cuisine on the ground floor.

Far-off, on the left side of the Champs Elysées, magnificent plane trees stand on the southeastern angle of the **GRAND PALAIS** (Great Palace). The **PETIT PALAIS** (Small Palace) and the Grand Palais are built for the 1900 World Fair.

*>> The statue of Winston Churchill*

Facing one another on both sides of the Churchill Avenue, these two buildings are constructed according to an eclectic architecture, very fashionable towards the end of the XIXth century : metallic structures and big glass roofs are associated with stone façades ornamented with classical decorative elements.

In an Art Nouveau style similar to the twin building facing it, the Petit Palais is built in 1900 by Charles Girault. It stands around a vast interior garden. From the big entrance hall, two long galleries stretch out leading to a pavilion heightened with a cupola. Today, it houses the Beaux-Arts museum of Paris City comprising three parts : Dutuit collections, Tuck collections and the Municipal collections constituted of French painters' art works from the XIXth century.

Built between 1897 and 1900, the Grand Palais is equally incorporated in the vast program of constructions for the 1900 World Fair. The architects Deglane, Louvet and Thomas designed the façades, drawn in an extremely academic style. Behind the ionic colonnade and

>> *Le Grand Palais, and its garden below*

the walls of its big hall, highlighted by mosaic friezes, the building deploys a stairway under a big cupola of 43 meters height.

The decoration is particularly well kept, from the quadrigae of angle perrons to Modern Style paintings. In fact, the project aims at classifying the building as a « monument devoted by the Republic for the glory of French Art ».

The 35,000 square meters surface area allow this palace to house numerous and diverse manifestations. Between 1900 and 1937, it annually welcomes the « Salon des Oeuvres d'Art Contemporain » (Exhibition of Contemporary Art Works), and the « Salon de l'Automobile » (Car exhibition) as well as the « Salon des Arts Ménagers » (Domestic arts exhibition). Today, it serves as a setting for the Palais de la Découverte (Discovery Palace) and houses temporary art exhibitions, thanks to the restoration of the galleries in 1964-1966. A part of the Grand Palais is closed for security reasons in 1993; its glass roofs are currently under restoration.

As to the **Palais de la Découverte**, it dynamically displays fundamental and contemporary science in the form of interactive experiences commented by presenters. Astronomy, with the new « Planetarium », biology, chemistry, mathematics, physics, and earth sciences are illustrated, in addition to the Electrostatics room and the Sun room. Reopening of the Acoustics room : it offers a series of experiments and demonstrations to investigate the sound phenomenon : sound propagation and speed, structure of simple and complex sounds (organ pipes), harmonic analysis and synthesis, interference and diffraction, Doppler Effect, beatings, resonance, etc.

*>> The pediment of the Palais de la Découverte*

In the angle of the two palaces, stands the magnificent **Pont Alexandre III** (Alexander III Bridge). The construction of this bridge was decided in 1896, due to traffic jams, the building of the Invalides railroad station (1893), and most of all, the project was re-launched because of the prospect of the World Fair. As a symbol of the French Russian alliance, the first stone was laid down by the Tsar Nicolas II of Russia, son of Alexander III. It was completed in 1900 and inaugurated at the occasion of the World Fair.

The Pont Alexandre III, classified as a historic monument in 1975, symbolizes the decorative spirit of the Belle-Époque. It represents an artistic testimony that characterizes architectural arts of the end of the XIXth century. With the Grand and Petit Palais, it is one of the rare works of monumental urban planning, having survived the 1900 World Fair. It is also the largest bridge of Paris.

*>> A detail of the Pont Alexandre III*

When coming back to the **CHAMPS-ELYSÉES**, one discovers the Champs-Elysées roundabout, drawn in 1670 but not landscaped until 1815. Then, one enters the green zone of the « Champs ». Hittorff rehabilitated the Champs-Elysées gardens between 1830 and 1840. He was the designer of Ledoyen and Laurent restaurants, the only pavilions we were able to uncover from that epoch. The site was then very popular and the Parisians were fond of these « panoramas », collections of paintings that incite true sensations for viewers placed at the center of this landscape at 360 degrees. The Rond-Point Theatre (Roundabout Theater) elected domicile in one of these old panoramas built by Davioud around 1860. It was revived during the eighties by the installation of the Renaud Barrault Company.

When going up the Avenue des « Champs », one can see in the vicinity of Gaumont-Marignan (n° 27), a number of plaques signed by movie celebrities (Michèle Morgan, Claude Lelouch, Agnès Varda, etc.) and affixed to the sidewalk on the occasion of the Movie Festival of Paris in 2000. The Hotel de la Païva (n° 25) is built around 1860 for Thérèse Lackman : this extremely opportunist woman left Moscow and moved to Paris where she married the Marquis of Païva y Araujo before falling for an immensely wealthy count, close to Bismarck, who allows him to turn this modest residence into the most beautiful private mansion in Paris. It is designed by Pierre Manguin and decorated by Carrier-Belleuse, Dalou and Baudry.

While walking up « Les Champs » on the sidewalk with uneven numbers, one passes by Le Fouquet's (n° 99), an establishment which was the first restaurant in the avenue since 1840, but which bears its current name since 1901. This place is frequented by all showbiz celebrities and is classified amongst Historic Monuments since 1991. Before reaching the Place de l'Etoile (Etoile Square), one goes by Publicis drugstore (n° 133), founded in 1962 and rebuilt after the fire of 1972.

At the top of the Champs Elysées, the Arc de Triomphe (Triumph Arch) of the place de l'Etoile (Etoile Square) is the most illustrious symbol of the History of France. Decorated on all its facades with sculpted collections, « le départ des volontaires » (the departure of volunteers), facing the Champs Elysées, seems to invite you to visit it. At more than fifty meters above the ground, you would overlook Parisian life and gaze at the renowned perspectives of Parisian urban planners, amongst which ranks first Baron Haussman.

*>> The Arc de Triomphe, Place de l'Étoile*

In the heart of the swarming Parisian life, in a quarter where the business world mingles with that of trade and tourism, the **ARC DE TRIOMPHE** of the Etoile, beyond its architectural and artistic value, is related to the collective unconscious of the French people. It constitutes an integral part of their monumental urban landscape and their national culture. You are invited to visit a monument where the past meets with the present.

Built as of 1806 by order of Napoleon I in honor of the French army and completed 30 years later under the reign of Louis Philippe, the Arc de Triomphe is both a memory and a symbol. You could not stand indifferent in front of this republican cathedral, which stood against all political upheavals. With its majestic architecture inspired by arches of antiquity, imagine yourself

witnessing the return of the emperor ashes in 1840 or the funeral of Victor Hugo in 1885. Moreover, you could not forget the passing by of victorious armies in 1919 and 1944. In the evening, after attending with emotion the revival of the Unknown Soldier's flame whose body rests under the arches since 1921, you could admire, from the terrace, the sun going down in front of you while Parisian lights plunge you into a dream world •

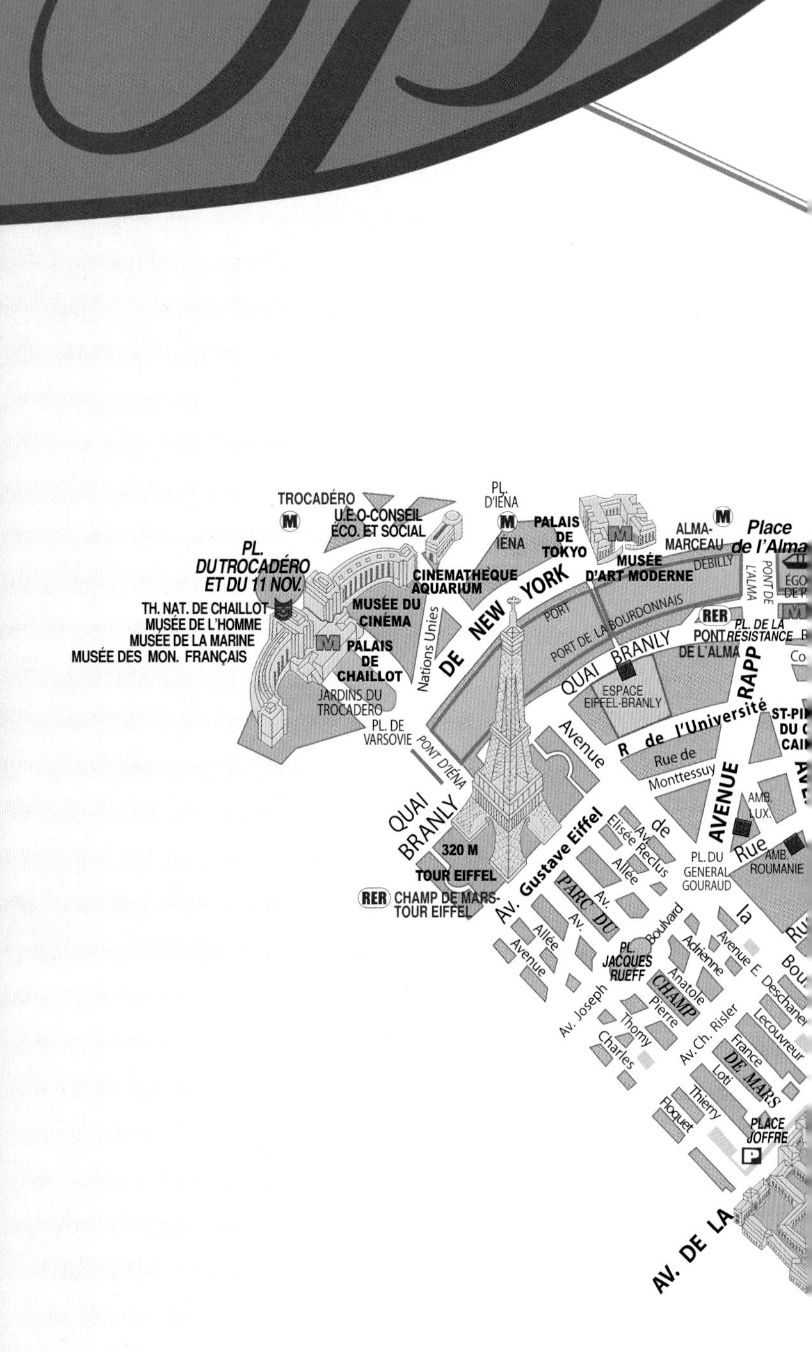
TROCADÉRO
U.E.O-CONSEIL ÉCO. ET SOCIAL
PL. D'IÉNA
IÉNA
PALAIS DE TOKYO
MUSÉE D'ART MODERNE
ALMA-MARCEAU
Place de l'Alma
PL. DU TROCADÉRO ET DU 11 NOV.
TH. NAT. DE CHAILLOT
MUSÉE DE L'HOMME
MUSÉE DE LA MARINE
MUSÉE DES MON. FRANÇAIS
CINEMATHÈQUE AQUARIUM
MUSÉE DU CINÉMA
PALAIS DE CHAILLOT
JARDINS DU TROCADERO
PL. DE VARSOVIE
PONT D'IÉNA
Nations Unies
DE NEW YORK
PORT
PORT DE LA BOURDONNAIS
DEBILLY
PONT DE L'ALMA
RER
PL. DE LA RÉSISTANCE
PONT DE L'ALMA
QUAI BRANLY
ESPACE EIFFEL-BRANLY
RAPP
R de l'Université
Rue de Monttessuy
Avenue
AVENUE
AMB. LUX.
AMB. ROUMANIE
QUAI BRANLY
320 M
TOUR EIFFEL
RER CHAMP DE MARS-TOUR EIFFEL
Av. Gustave Eiffel
Av. Elisée Reclus
Allée
PARC DU
PL. DU GENERAL GOURAUD
Rue
la
Boulvard
Adrienne
Avenue E. Deschanel
PL. JACQUES RUEFF
Anatole
CHAMP
Pierre
Av. Joseph
Thomy
Charles
Av. Ch. Risler
France
Loti
DE MARS
Lecouvreur
Thierry
Floquet
PLACE JOFFRE
AV. DE LA

## •5th Itinerary•

# THE «INVALIDES» AND THE «CHAMP DE MARS»

## THE «INVALIDES» AND THE «CHAMP DE MARS»

On the left bank side, from the viewpoint of the pont de la Concorde (Concorde Bridge), the **ASSEMBLÉE NATIONALE** (National Assembly), also known as the Palais Bourbon (Bourbon Palace), is the seat of the French Parliament lower hall.

Architect Giardini starts the construction of this building in 1722, then Lassurance continus the works, and finally Aubert and Gabriel achieve it in 1728. It is originally built for the daughter of Louis XIV, the duchess of Bourbon who gave her name to the palace. In 1764, it becomes the property of prince de Condé, who expands it to its current aspect, imposing and noble, in the square bearing the same name.

From 1803 to1807, Napoleon assigns Poyet to build the façade overlooking the Seine in harmony with that of La Madeleine facing it, from afar, at the end of the Rue Royale (Royal Street). The façade portico holds an allegorical pediment sculpted by Cortot. Rude and Pradier did other allegorical bas-reliefs on the wings. The interior is rich in works of art. Thus, Delacroix decorated the Library with his fresco named « Histoire de la Civilisation » (History of Civilization), between 1838 and 1845, while Houdon sculpted the busts of Diderot and Voltaire for the same room. Considered at first as the seat of the « Conseil des Cinq Cents » (Council of the Five Hundred), then Chamber of Deputies, it houses today the Assemblée Nationale (National Assembly).

*>> On the left, the Eiffel Tower*
*>> Below, the Assemblée Nationale*

Not very far, when going up the rue de Lille, the Musée d'Orsay appears. Known in the whole world for its rich collection of impressionist art, the **MUSÉE D'ORSAY** is as well the museum of all artistic creations of the western world from 1848 to 1914. Its collections represent all forms of expression, from painting to architecture as well as sculpture, decorative arts and photography. The beauty of the place will no doubt dazzle you : a palace-like railway station inaugurated for the 1900 World Fair.

When going up towards the Assemblée Nationale (National Assembly), then following the Seine river, one crosses past the Pont Alexandre III which we already visited in the previous itinerary, until reaching the **PONT DES INVALIDES** (Invalides Bridge). At first, a one-arch suspended bridge is built in this location in 1826. The

engineers' lack of experience, added to a land settling, lead to the destruction of the bridge. It is replaced the following year by another 5-arch-suspended bridge, and again substituted by a stone bridge in 1854, that requires restoration as of 1878. For this reason, a provisional footbridge is erected upstream ; however, it tumbles down in January 1879, under the ice pressure. Swept along by the current, the debris causes the collapse of the bridge under reparation. Hence, it is fully rebuilt from 1879 to 1880. Pavements are enlarged in a corbelled construction in 1956.

*>> The Hôtel des Invalides*

Situated at the end of the Invalides esplanade, the **HÔTEL DES INVALIDES** is a majestic, immense monument built upon the initiative of Louis XIV. He personally lays the first stone on November 30, 1671.

The quadrilateral shaped hotel has impressive dimensions : 450 meters of length with 390 meters of width. The numerous internal courtyards and buildings stretch out on almost 10 hectares.

Two of the most famous architects of the epoch designed the building : the austere Libéral Bruant, from 1671 until 1674, to whom we owe the extraordinary 196 meter long facade, and the audacious Jules Hardouin-Mansart who takes after Bruant in 1676 and designs for the occasion the Church of the Dome.

One could start the visit by entering the « Jardin de l'Intendant » (Quartermaster Garden), a classical garden redesigned in 1980 with an XVIIIth Century style, including its pond, its flowerbeds studded with yew trees and its mall of lime trees.

>> *The Church of the Dome*

>> *The tomb of Lyautey*
>> *On the right, the Coupole*

The wonderful Church of the Dome, built between 1679 and 1706 by Jules Hardouin Mansart on a Greek cross shaped plan, dominates the place : the dome that surmounts it, with its openwork lantern culminating at 107 meters and the grand fresco under its cupola painted by Charles de la fosse, is a one of a kind ever built in France. On the occasion of the bicentenary of the French Revolution, the dome is re-gilded it in 1989 for the fifth time since its creation, hence, this operation necessitates the use of 12.65 kg of the precious metal, i.e. 550,000 gold leafs of 0.2 micron of thickness. Real military pantheon with the tombs housing the heart of Vauban, the remains of Turenne, the heart of Tour d'Auvergne ; the Dome mainly embraces the tomb of Napoleon the first, the sepulchers of his brothers Joseph and Jérôme Bonaparte, of his son, the king of Rome, those of generals Bertrand and Duroc, and marshals Foch and Lyautey.

A windowpane separates the church of the Dome from Saint-Louis-des-Invalides, also referred to as Soldiers Church, built by Libéral Bruant. On the left side of the Church of the Dome appears the entrance of the gigantic Musée de l'Armée (Army Museum), founded in 1905, fruit of the fusion between the Artillery Museum and the historic museum of the Army itself established a hundred years later, after the World Fair.

The museum keeps, on a 8000 square meters area, a collection of 500,000 listed items, amongst which the armor of François 1st, the pistol of Charles V in addition to many other weapons and uniforms that have witnessed the prestigious military past of France.

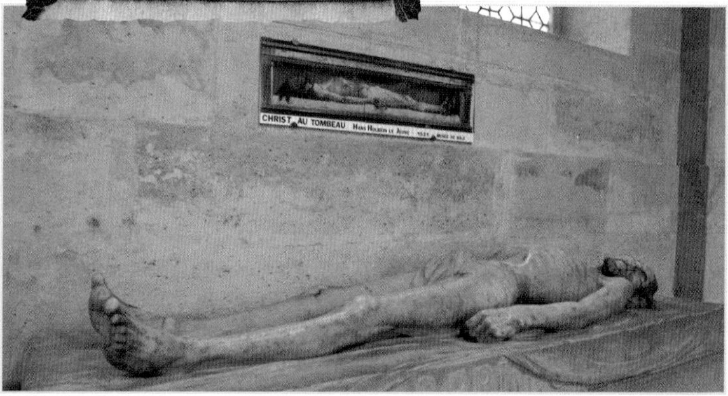

>> *Christ au Tombeau (Christ Entombed)*

These data render the museum one of the most important museums of military history in France and one of the very first in the world. The museum's permanent collections are divided into the so-called « historic » collections, corresponding to a circuit of chronological presentation form the antiquity till the end of World War II, enriched with items belonging to « thematic » series (emblems, paintings, decorations…).

Hence, these thematic collections are displayed all along the historic rooms, or in specific areas : for instance, the Turenne room comprises emblems ; and the Gribeauval room small models of artillery.

A must-see site is the surprising museum of the Plans Reliefs, designed since 1777 in the attics of the Invalides around the collection created by Louis XIV. Its models of ports and fortified towns allowed the King's strategists to simulate sieges and attacks.

One can walk out of the museum through a large courtyard of honor, 102 meters long and 63 meters wide, on a total area of 6.426 square meters, with galleries lined by numerous cannons.

In the Santiago-du-Chili square, two impressive Oriental plane trees dominate a splendid green area of 3,300 square meters designed in 1865 and filled with various scents : Lime trees, chestnut trees, maples and exotic trees. The terrace preceding the long façade of the Hotel des Invalides is decorated with cannons taken from the King of Prussia, Frederic II.

On the other side, bordering the boulevard of the Invalides, the Ajaccio square is designed by Alphand in 1865. It contains a 150 years old oriental plane tree. Robert de Cotte drew the esplanade of the Invalides in 1704 on one part of the « Pré aux Clercs » (Cleric meadow) location. The esplanade's vastness is in perfect harmony with the splendor of the hotel it precedes : 487 meters long and 250 meters wide. It mainly provides a remarkable view of the Pont Alexandre-III and the squat silhouettes of the Petit and Grand Palais. Bordered by Lime trees, different paths streamline with the six-grassed flowerbeds, packed during summer months by Parisians who seek relaxation.

*>> The courtyard of the Invalides*

Nearby the Invalides, the **MUSÉE RODIN** (Rodin Museum) gathers Works and collections of the sculptor Auguste Rodin in this XVIIIth century private mansion, built by architects Jacques Gabriel and Jean Auber. Some of the sculptor's great masterpieces are exhibited in the park, amongst which the famous « Penseur » (thinker).

*>> The zouave of the Pont de l'Alma*

On the way to the Seine, the **PONT DE L'ALMA** (Alma Bridge) is situated. It is one of the most famous bridges of Paris, mainly due to its zouave, indicator of rise in the water level. Hence, in 1910, the water went up to the beard's statue. A first bridge was constructed in this location around 1855 by Napoleon III who names it after his first victory in Crimea, on September 20, 1854.

Four statutes of soldiers embellished then the bridge's piles. The zouave quickly attracts Parisians' liking, at the expense of the artilleryman, the grenadier and the hunter. The work of Georges Diebolt was the only one preserved during the bridge reconstruction, between May 1970 and June 1974.

When crossing the Rapp Avenue, the **CHAMPS DE MARS** greets you. It is situated at the feet of the Eiffel Tower where gardens are laid out, mainly a floral garden.

The rectilinear shape of the Champ de Mars is a reminder of the initial purpose of the land : a parade ground for the Military School. Opened in 1780, it becomes a high place for national events : The Federation's day in 1790, the presentation of decorations by Napoleon I in 1804, it then starts hosting many World Fairs.

>> *The Champ de Mars*

Lakes, ponds, sinuous paths and other grottos embellish the Champ de Mars. Various birds visit this place, one of the rarest in Paris where the singing of the tawny owl echoes at night.

Towering over the Champs de Mars, the **Tour Eiffel** (Eiffel Tower) is the first archetype of a giant iron structure. It is designed and executed by the architect and builder Gustave Eiffel for the Paris World Fair in 1889.

>> *The Bust of Gustave Eiffel*

The tower measures 312 meters of height, without its Hertzian broadcasting antenna. When taking the latter into consideration, it reached 324 meters ever since the antenna restoration works were carried out in January 2001. Before this date, it was only 318.70 meters high, from the time when the first TV broadcasting antenna was positioned in 1957.

Four arched pillars fixed on four small blocked up structures support the tower. As they go up, the arches are set upright and then blend at the second floor level in a unique streamlined caisson.

The tower has three platforms, each offering a panoramic viewpoint. The first platform also has a restaurant.

The tower weighs around 7,300 tons, excluding foundations, fixtures and fittings, which represents a very small load of 4 kg per square centimeter of foundations.

In close proximity to the top, a meteorological station and a radio communication station are positioned : the first tests of radio (1898) and TV broadcasting (1925) were carried out from the tower's top. The place also houses Gustave Eiffel's laboratory, destined for tests on wind resistance, however, this lab is moved to Rue Boileau in Paris, in 1921.

*>> The sunset in Paris*

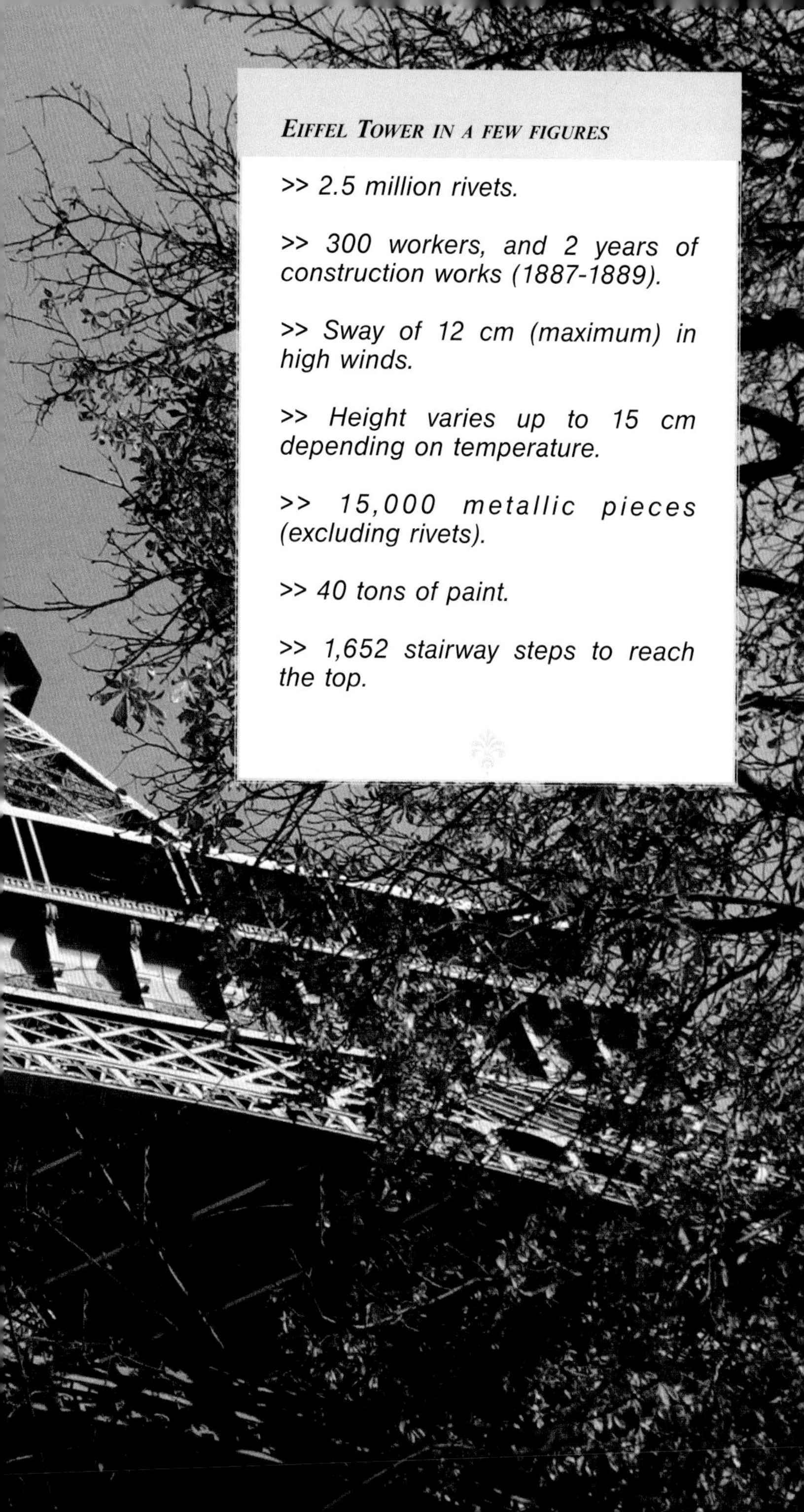

## Eiffel Tower in a few figures

>> 2.5 million rivets.

>> 300 workers, and 2 years of construction works (1887-1889).

>> Sway of 12 cm (maximum) in high winds.

>> Height varies up to 15 cm depending on temperature.

>> 15,000 metallic pieces (excluding rivets).

>> 40 tons of paint.

>> 1,652 stairway steps to reach the top.

In the same axis of the Champ de Mars, the **Pont d'Iéna** (Iena Bridge) crosses the Seine River. It is Napoleon Ist who initiated the construction of a bridge in the axis of the Champ de Mars. This bridge was supposed to bear the name of « Pont du Champ de Mars », nevertheless the emperor decides to name it after the victory he had just achieved in 1806.

At the fall of the empire in 1815, Prussians want to demolish the bridge because of its name. The Pont d'Iéna is then renamed « Pont des Invalides » and the royal initial « L » replaces the imperial eagles. The construction of the bridge begins in 1808 and is not completed until 1814. The building costs are provided by the state, which constitutes a new happening for that epoch. The Iena Bridge soon becomes insufficient in terms of capacity and is enlarged in 1937 from 19 to 35 meters for the occasion of the World Fair.

Facing the Pont d'Iéna (Iena Bridge), the **Trocadéro** dominates the Chaillot hill. In the XVIth century, Catherine de Medicis commissions the construction of a country cottage on the Chaillot hill, acquired later by the Maréchal of Bassompière.

In 1651, queen Henriette of England buys the castle in order to found the convent of the Visitation, where numerous famous Ladies come to withdraw from society. The convent is later razed in order to erect the palace that Napoleon dreams of building for his son, the king of Rome. However, his dream is shattered by the fall of the Empire.

>> *Wing of the Trocadéro*

The Trocadéro derives its name from the fortress of Cadix occupied by the French in 1823 in order to reestablish the absolute monarchy in Spain. The Trocadéro Palace, which architecture is inspired from the Moresque art, is built for the Universal Exhibition of 1878. The current Palais de Chaillot is reconstructed on the site of the same Palace for the occasion of the Universal Exhibition of 1937.

The architects Azema, Carlu, and Boileau designed the current Palais de Chaillot. It has the shape of two curved wings sliding towards the Seine. Between these two wings, the esplanade of human rights overlooks the Tour Eiffel and the Champs de Mars. The Palais de Chaillot houses several museums, among which the « musée de l'homme » (Museum of Mankind), along with the museums of the cinema, of the Marine as well as the film library.

>> *The Palais de Chaillot*

>> *The Eiffel Tower seen from the Trocadéro*

The World Fair of 1937 was also the reason for building the **Musée d'Art Moderne** de la ville de Paris (Museum of Modern Art of Paris City), a few cables' length away from the Tocadéro. This museum, which occupies half of Palais de Tokyo (Tokyo Palace), is officially inaugurated in 1961. Permanent collections illustrate most of the XXth century's European and French Art currents, from Fauvism to the contemporary creation with its most diverse disciplines, going through Cubism, the School of Paris, Abstraction-Creation, Lyric Abstraction, New Realism, Support Surface, Povera Art, Conceptual Art...

The « historic » section organizes temporary exhibitions dedicated to determining movements, or to artists who have marked the XXth century and soon the XXIst century. In parallel, the contemporary section offers in-depth information covering the national and international current events through monographic or thematic exhibitions and reveals young talents, as well as the most innovative research •

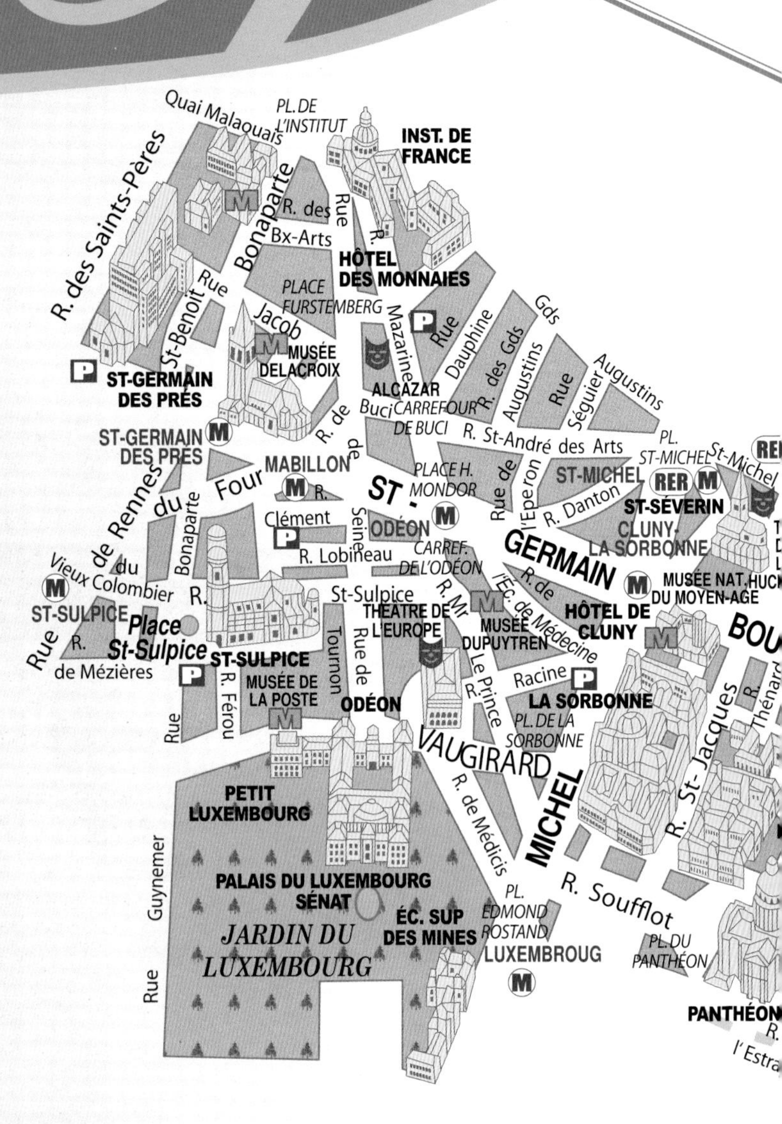

Quai Malaquais
PL. DE L'INSTITUT
INST. DE FRANCE
R. des Saints-Pères
Bonaparte
R. des Bx-Arts
Rue
R.
HÔTEL DES MONNAIES
Rue St-Benoit
PLACE FURSTEMBERG
Jacob
MUSÉE DELACROIX
Mazarine
Rue Dauphine
R. des Gds Augustins
Gds Augustins
Rue Séguier
ST-GERMAIN DES PRÉS
ALCAZAR
CARREFOUR DE BUCI
R. de Buci
R. St-André des Arts
PL. ST-MICHEL
St-Michel
ST-GERMAIN DES PRÉS
MABILLON
R. de Seine
PLACE H. MONDOR
Rue de l'Eperon
ST-MICHEL
RER
Rue de Rennes
du Four
R. Clément
ST-ODÉON
R. Danton
ST-SÉVERIN
CLUNY-LA SORBONNE
Bonaparte
R. Lobineau
CARREF. DE L'ODÉON
GERMAIN
R. du Vieux Colombier
R. St-Sulpice
R. de l'Éc. de Médecine
MUSÉE NAT. DU MOYEN-AGE
ST-SULPICE
Place St-Sulpice
THÉATRE DE L'EUROPE
MUSÉE DUPUYTREN
HÔTEL DE CLUNY
R. de Mézières
ST-SULPICE
Rue de Tournon
R. Mr Le Prince
Racine
R. Férou
MUSÉE DE LA POSTE
ODÉON
LA SORBONNE
PL. DE LA SORBONNE
R. St-Jacques
R. Thénard
Rue
VAUGIRARD
PETIT LUXEMBOURG
R. de Médicis
MICHEL
Rue Guynemer
PALAIS DU LUXEMBOURG SÉNAT
R. Soufflot
PL. EDMOND ROSTAND
JARDIN DU LUXEMBOURG
ÉC. SUP DES MINES
LUXEMBROUG
PL. DU PANTHÉON
PANTHÉON
R. l'Estra

# •6th Itinerary•

## «Saint Germain des Prés» and the «Quartier Latin»

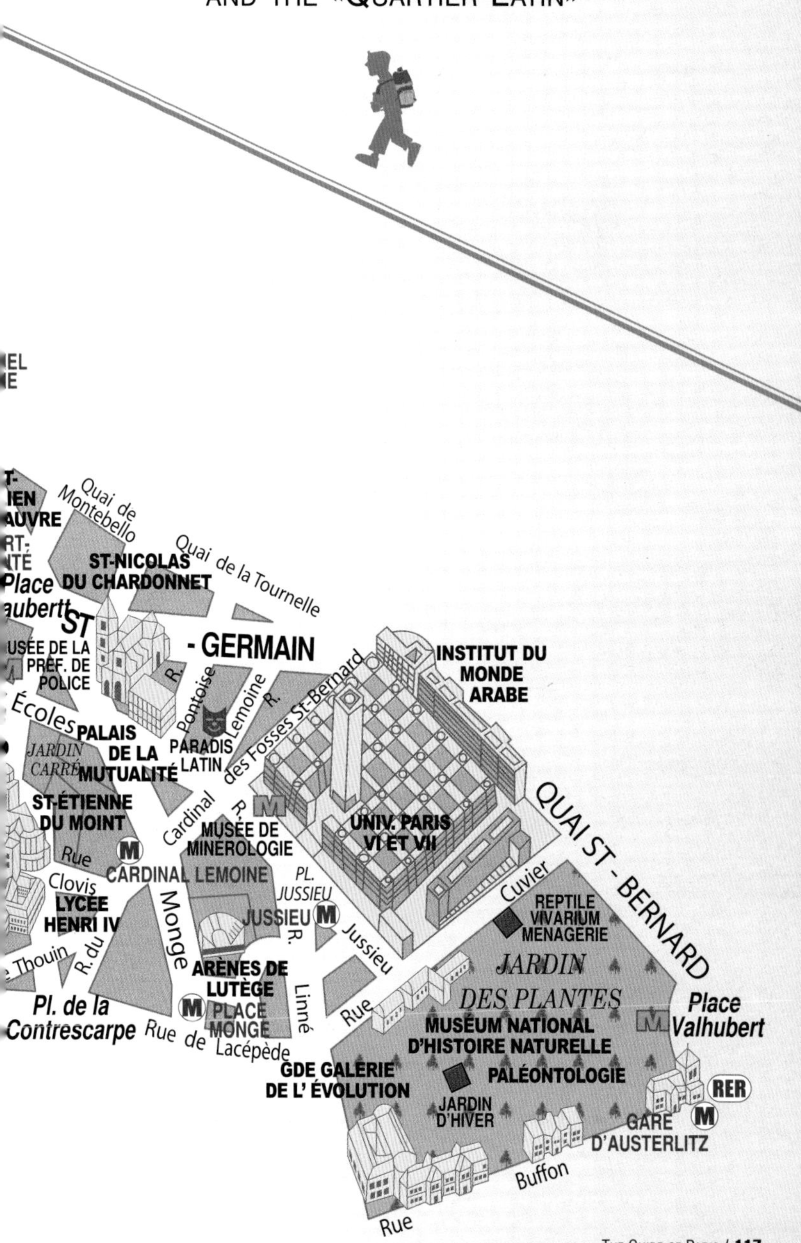

# Saint Germain des Prés and the quartier Latin (Latin Quarter)

This quarter, situated on the left bank, originates from the extension of a village that was formed around the **Church of Saint Germain des Prés**, the most ancient of major Churches in Paris.

The church is founded in the VIth century by the Merovingian King Childebert. He decides to build the Basilica of Sainte-Croix (Sacred Cross) and Saint-Vincent, which shall house the relics and tombs of Merovingian Kings.

In 558, the burial of Childebert coincides with the consecration of the basilica by Saint-Germain, the bishop of Paris. In the IXth century, the Vikings ruin the abbey ; hence, the current edifice is built only towards the end of the Xth century. Monks from the Benedictine order shall settle in the abbey, which vast agricultural field covered the two current 6th and 7th arrondissements.

*>> The fountain of the Saint Sulpice church*

In the year one thousand, under the reign of Robert le Pieux (Robert the Pious), the abbot Morard undertakes the reconstruction works : the tower, nave, Saint Symborien Chapel and apse. In 1163, Pope Alexander III consecrates the new choir, the old having become too old.

Significantly restored in the XVIIth century by the Maurists, who endow it with an extraordinary spiritual blossoming, the abbey becomes a parish, composed of a Roman nave, a transept and a chorus with five glowing chapels.

On its occidental facade, it has a Gothic portal as well as a bell-tower, one of the oldest in France, which first three floors date back to earlier than 1014.

As to the Saint-Germain-des-Prés quarter, it bears witness of an important intellectual life, as it comprises a Faculty of Medicine, an Art School, as well as famous literary brasseries and cafés such as the « Procop », one of the oldest cafés of Paris where several literary and political generations used to gather, starting with Voltaire and the

encyclopedia writers, or the « Deux Magots », the brasserie « Lipp », the « Flore », all of which are extremely visited by post-war intellectuals such as Malraux, Camus, Prévert, Sartre, Simone de Beauvoir, Juliette Gréco…

When going up the Saint Germain Boulevard, then taking the rue du Four on the right, then the rue Bonaparte directly on the left, the Place Saint Sulpice (Saint Sulpice Square) appears, where a church bearing the same name is situated.

On the current location of the **EGLISE SAINT SULPICE** (Saint Sulpice Church), a parochial church is built in the IXth century. It belongs to the neighboring abbey of Saint Germain des Prés, which we evoked earlier

Rebuilt between the XIIIth and XVth century, it formed then a charming gothic edifice, with engravings that preserved its silhouette. However, in the XVIIth century, it was evident that it had become insufficient. Thus, in 1642, the new parish priest, Jean-Jacques Olier, founder of the famous seminar and the religious congregation of Saint Sulpice, decides to reconstruct his church on the designs of architect Christophe Gamard. The duke of Orleans lays the first stone of the edifice in 1646. Gamard dies in 1665 and is replaced by Louis Le Vau, himself succeeded by Daniel Gittard in 1670. In 1675, the Virgin's Chapel, the choir along with its ambulatory are finalized when the works of the transept's square and the north crosspiece are started.

The interior reproduces the design and reaches the dimensions of a medieval cathedral with its 5-bay-nave adjoined by aisles and chapels, its vast transept, its choir with two straight ways, and its three sided hemicycle, surrounded by an ambulatory and chapels. The following are the measurements of this magnificent vessel : 120 meters length, 57 meters large, 30 meters height under the central vault. Its decoration style is influenced by Italy but its monumental design is authentically French.

Two vast antique porticos from the facade, the first has of Doric style while the other has a Corinthian style, both surmounted by a vast triangular pediment between two towers. On the church's square stands a fountain designated as the « four bishops » for Massillon, Fléchier, Fénelon, and Bossuet. It is designed by the architect Ludovico Visconti.

The Saint-Sulpice church is one of the biggest and mostly decorated Jesuit style churches. It is also one of the most visited churches of Paris. It has gained an enormous notoriety lately since the release of the best-seller « Da Vinci Code », as it represents one the places of intrigue of this book.

Not far off, the **PALAIS DU LUXEMBOURG** (Luxembourg Palace) houses the Sénat (Senate) which is the French parliament's supreme chamber since 1958.
The site that embraces today the Gardens and the Palace of Luxembourg was originally a Roman camp. In 1257, when the Chartreux family settled in, this lavish place was a disreputable spot to a point where it was considered as cursed. The Chartreux family transformed it into a flourishing convent.

In 1612, Marie de Medicis buys the hotel owned by the Duc de Luxembourg and builds, in 1615, her own palace designed by Salomon de Brosse in a Renaissance style, reminding her of her native Tuscany. Although she was sent into exile, the palace remained the property of the royal family until the Revolution. The gardens are extended over the Chartreux family land and offer today a splendid panorama for walkers.

The **JARDINS DU LUXEMBOURG** (Luxembourg Garden) is undoubtedly amongst the greatest gardens of the capital, with a surface area of 25 hectares.

*>> The view from the Luxembourg Gardens*

The concept of a public park, distinct from the princely garden, which was open to the public by kindness of the owners, did not prevail before the end of the second empire. The ultimate right of access was not granted to the « common herd » until the Count of Provence (future Louis XVIII) became owner of the Luxembourg Palace. For a reasonable admission charge, one could have cold drinks and eat freshly picked fruits.

The Luxembourg Garden comprises various monuments and statues. The most famous is the « Medicis fountain » surmounted by a pediment bearing the queen weaponry. It is most likely an artwork by Salomon de Brosse, built in the style of Italian grottos. While walking towards the big pond, do not miss the « masks merchant » achieved by Zacharie Asturc in 1883, which pedestal is surrounded by masks of Corot, Dumas, Carpeaux, Fauré, Delacroix, Balzac, and Barbier d'Aurevilly.

Much visited by inhabitants of the quarter, the Luxembourg was the favorite place for great writers, amongst which Baudelaire, Lamartine, Musset, Verlaine, Victor Hugo, George Sand, Balzac, Hemingway and Sartre.

Beehives, rose gardens, and fruit trees are a reminiscence of the horticultural tradition of the Chartreux family and of the plant nursery that was located in the present Rue Auguste Comte before Haussman's restoration works.

Facing the northern entry to the Luxembourg garden, the **PANTHEON** overlooks Mount Saint-Genevieve. In the middle of the Latin Quarter with its schools and universities, the Pantheon towers over all Paris.

During almost all the XIXth Century, far before the Eiffel Tower, the Sacré-Coeur of Montmartre or the Montparnasse Tower, the Pantheon was the first monument that every foreigner arriving to Paris would see, and on top of which one could have a true panoramic view of the city.

The Basilica of Sainte Genevieve, which became the Pantheon during the French revolution, constitutes a masterpiece of architecture of the late XVIIIth century as well as a living witness of the History of France for more than 250 years.

According to a scholar of the Enlightenment Century, the Pantheon is considered a model of achievement combining « the subtlety of the construction of Gothic edifices and the purity and magnificence of the Greek architecture ». Masterpiece of the Architect Soufflot, the Pantheon is a part of the renewal of the Parisian urban planning, which makes it a « must see » site while visiting the monuments of the capital.

Thanks to its location at the top of Mount Saint-Genevieve, it is a reference point in the city and remains for all people the spirit of the Latin Quarter. Famous for its dome, which is an admirable synthesis of balance, in perfect harmony, this edifice is also known for its interior design. Due to contradictory allocations of this monument since the Revolution, the design combines Christian and Republican symbols in a great ideological confusion. Deemed as a church, a temple of humanity or a national basilica according to the regimes, the paintings located on the lower sides of the nave reflect, through the intensity of the message they communicate, the artistic syncretism of the IIIrd Republic, namely that of Puvis de Chavanne.

Beyond the impression of power the building conveys, the Pantheon became today, first and foremost, a republican necropolis where the History of France merges with the world of writers, scientists, generals, ecclesiastics and politicians... Furthermore, after stepping across the entrance peristyle, the visitor cannot but spend some moments in silence in front of the solemnity of the spaces and remain astounded by the immensity of the premises. The swaying of the pendulum placed at the center of the building, which is a replica of the Foucault experiment of 1851 to establish the earth's circular shape, is the only sound that seems to disturb the deep hovering quietude. The crypt houses the tombs of more than 70 important figures including Voltaire, Jean-Jacques Rousseau and even Alexandre Dumas buried on November 28, 2002.

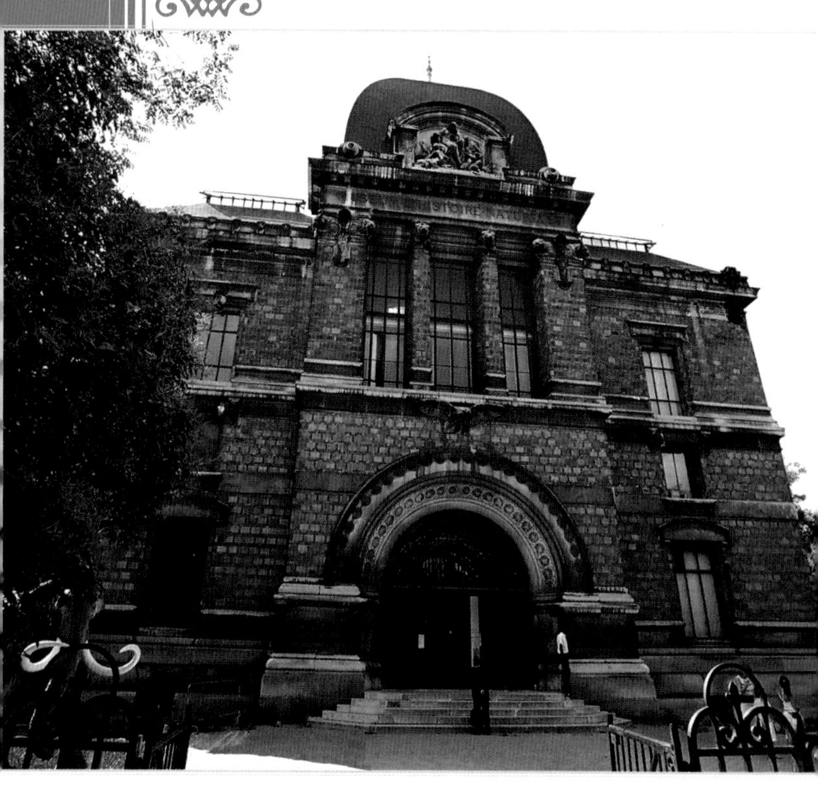

At the bottom of mount Saint Genevieve, the **MUSÉUM D'HISTOIRE NATURELLE** (Museum of Natural History) is established in 1635 and is named then the « Jardin royal des plantes médicinales » (Royal garden of medicinal plants). It becomes the national museum of natural history in 1793, with the same missions that it still carries on today in the fields of natural and human sciences : the preservation and enrichment of collections, fundamental and applied research, teaching and spreading knowledge to all categories of people.

The museum is one of the world's three institutions that comprise the greatest number of collections related to nature. Besides constituting a heritage of universal value, these

collections allow researchers to make the inventory of our planet's biodiversity.

Names of great scholars are attached to this museum and numerous scientific discoveries mark out the history of this establishment. This is where Buffon, Geoffroy Saint-Hilaire, Cuvier, Lamarck, Sebastien Vaillant discover the plants' sexuality, Claude Bernard substantiates his discoveries pertinent to the liver's glycogenetic function, and René-Just Haüy establishes the fundamental laws of crystallography.

In 1896, Henri Becquerel, professor at the laboratory of applied physics and a luminescence specialist, same as his father Edmond Becquerel, discovers the « uranic rays » on the first floor of the small building that embraces the Botanical Garden and overlooks the rue Cuvier.

Nowadays, the discoveries of Becquerel, in addition to those of Marie & Pierre Curie find their application and serve the research of multiple laboratories of the museum in mineralogy, physical oceanography, paleontology, pre-history, chemistry, biophysics, and molecular biology •

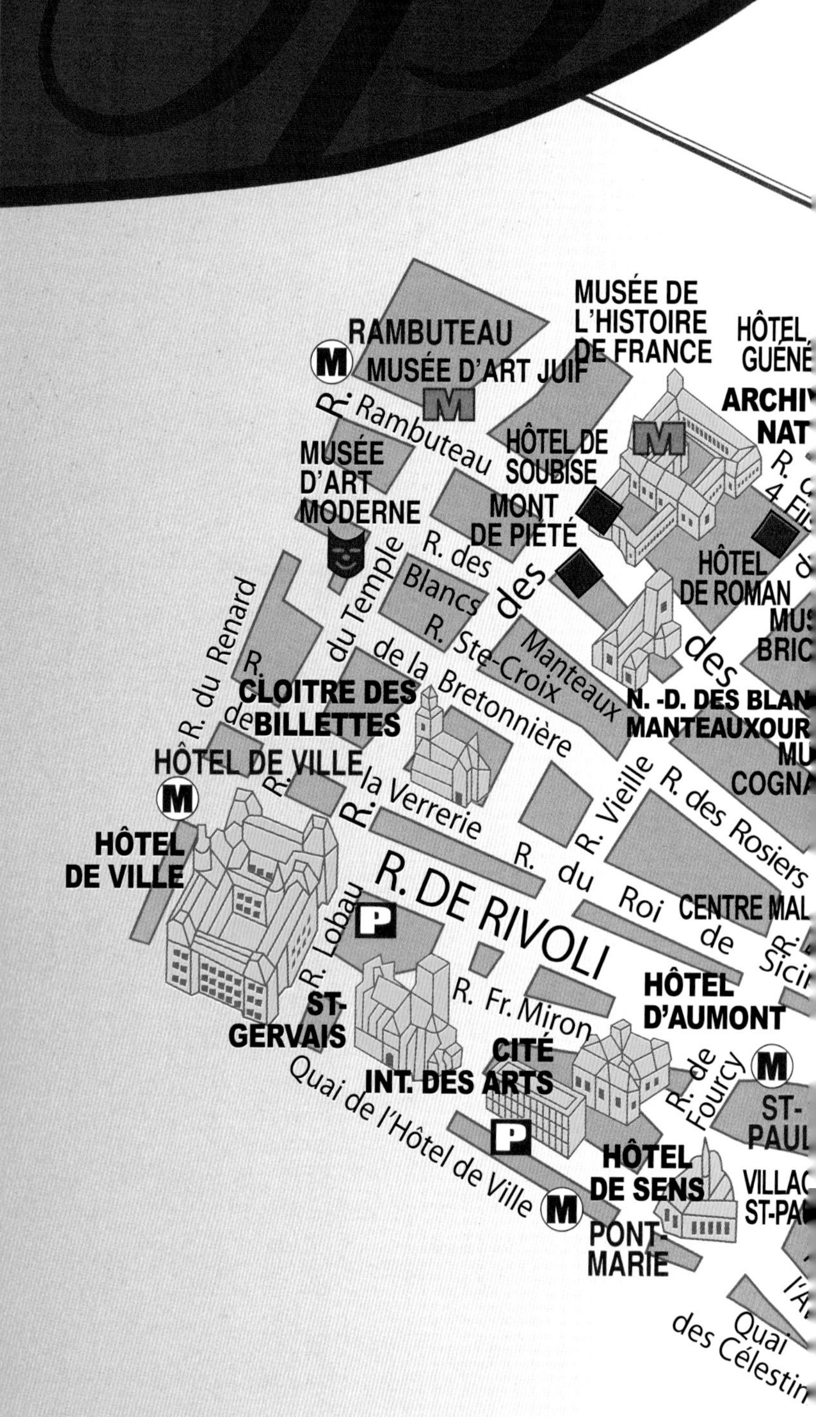
RAMBUTEAU
MUSÉE D'ART JUIF
MUSÉE DE
L'HISTOIRE
DE FRANCE
R. Rambuteau
MUSÉE
D'ART
MODERNE
HÔTEL DE
SOUBISE
MONT
DE PIÉTÉ
R. des
Blancs
R. du Temple
des
Manteaux
R. Ste-Croix
de la Bretonnière
R. du Renard
R.
CLOITRE DES
de BILLETTES
HÔTEL DE VILLE
R. de la Verrerie
HÔTEL
DE VILLE
R. DE RIVOLI
R. Lobau
R. Vieille
R. des Rosiers
R. du Roi de Sicil
HÔTEL
D'AUMONT
R. Fr. Miron
ST-
GERVAIS
CITÉ
INT. DES ARTS
R. de Fourcy
Quai de l'Hôtel de Ville
HÔTEL
DE SENS
PONT-
MARIE
HÔTEL DE ROMAN
N. -D. DES BLAN
MANTEAUX
CENTRE MAL
Quai
des Célestin

# •7th Itinerary•

## DISCOVER THE «MARAIS»

LIBERTÉ
ÉGALITÉ
FRATERNITÉ

# DISCOVERING THE MARAIS

Very early on, the Cité (City), cradle of Paris, is short of space between the two arms of the Seine River. On the Seine's right bank, flat lands are inundated by every flood of the river, the marais (swamps).

The Marais emerges as a quarter of the XIVth century. When King Charles V settles in the hotel St-Pol instead of the Palais de la Cité (City Palace), this induces the enlargement of the Eastern fortifications of the city and the inclusion of the neighboring cultivated swamps. The new royal district rapidly attracts great Lords and merchants ; it also abounds with luxurious hotels. This urbanization shall carry on for three centuries until reaching its peak under Henry IV with namely the construction of the Place Royale (Royal square), the current Place des Vosges (Vosges square).

In the XVIIIth century, the great bourgeoisie goes into exile towards the West to get closer to Versailles, leaving the place for craftsmen and provincials. After the revolution, the convents and big mansions that had become national properties are destroyed or parceled for profitability purposes. The industrial revolution ends up transforming the quarter which slowly plunges into insalubrity.

The future of the Marais is not seriously considered before the 1930s. The modernists that preach the eradication of buildings and the construction of towers, such as Le Corbusier, are opposed to the Giovannoni School, fervent adherent to renovation. This last idea shall be imposed with the Malraux law of 1962 regarding the protection of urban areas. Since then, the quarter has sprung up again and recovered its charm and renowned activity.

*>> The Hôtel de Ville, front side and statue*

Enclosed by the Rue de Rivoli on one side and the Seine River on the other, the Hotel de Ville square is entirely dominated by the large facade of the **HÔTEL DE VILLE**.

The Hotel de Ville which houses the town hall of Paris is an edifice built in 1882 in a Renaissance style based on the design of the old Hotel de Ville set on fire during the events of the Commune in 1871.

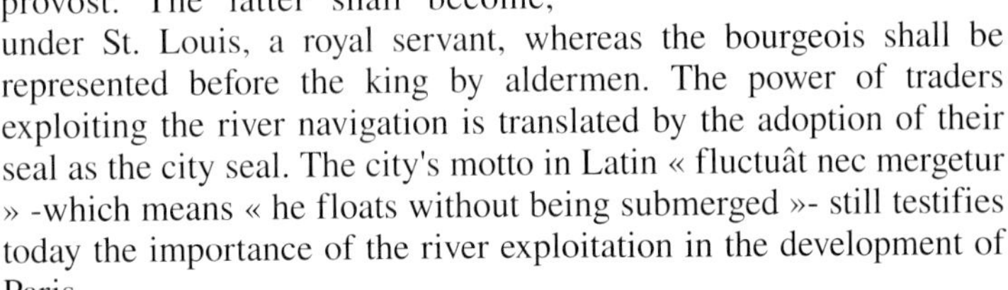

The growing importance of the bourgeoisie in the Middle Ages gives birth to a new type of city administration headed by a provost. The latter shall become, under St. Louis, a royal servant, whereas the bourgeois shall be represented before the king by aldermen. The power of traders exploiting the river navigation is translated by the adoption of their seal as the city seal. The city's motto in Latin « fluctuât nec mergetur » -which means « he floats without being submerged »- still testifies today the importance of the river exploitation in the development of Paris.

During the Middle Ages, the municipality was established at the Place de Grève (Grève square) in a building named at that epoch « Maison des Piliers » (House of Pillars), purchased by Etienne Marcel, the provost of Paris. In the XVIth century, François 1st commands the architect Dominique de Cortone, named Boccador, to erect a new building for the municipality.

The Hotel de Ville was the scene of many political events, mainly when Louis XVI received the tricolor rosette on July 17, 1789. On September 4, 1870, the Republic was proclaimed in the Hotel de Ville before the edifice was set on fire.

*>> The statue in the front side of the Hôtel de Ville*

The interior designs are a reflection of receptions given at the Hotel de Ville.

>> *The equestrian statue of Louis XIII*

In the heart of the Marais, the **PLACE DES VOSGES** (Vosges square), is a perfect square of 108 meter sides, surrounded by trees and flower-beds, as well as a marble statue of Louis XIII on a horse, a copy of P Biard's destroyed during the Revolution.

*>> The entrance door of one of the pavilions, Place des Vosges*

The origin of this square dates back to 1559, when Henri II gets injured during a tournament and is transported to the Hotel des Tournelles where he passes away. Thus, Catherine de Medicis decides to destroy the hotel. Later on, Henri IV starts building a square originally intended to house silk manufactories. The works are completed in 1612.

The Vosges square is composed of thirty six pavilions-nine on each side-among which are the king's and the Queen's pavilions built firstly. The square rapidly becomes a trendy place ; hence, the noblemen of the Royal Court start building sumptuous residences.

>> *The fountain of the square Louis XIII, Place des Vosges*

Initially known as Place Royale, it bears the name of Place des Vosges around 1800 to pay tribute to the first department that acquitted its taxes.

Victor Hugo resides for almost 16 years at n° 6 of the Place des Vosges where one can visit today his mansion.

Not far off, on n°5 of the rue de Thorigny in the Hôtel Salé (Salted Hotel), the **MUSÉE PICASSO** (Picasso Museum) gathers works of Picasso which the Government donated after the death of the artist, as well as the personal collection of Pablo Picasso. The Hotel Salé was built from 1656 to 1659 for Pierre Aubert, farmer of the Gabelles, who was in charge of collecting taxes on salt.

*>> The courtyard of the Carnavalet Museum*

On n°23 of rue Sévigné, the **MUSÉE CARNAVALET** (Carnavalet Museum), was inaugurated in 1880. This museum is dedicated to the History of Paris, from its origins to our present days.

It features, in the hotels Carnavalet and Le Peletier de Saint-Fargeau, exceptional collections exhibited in the halls which reproduce the atmosphere of private residences of the XVth and XIXth centuries : archeological Gallo-Roman and Medieval background, souvenirs of the French Revolution, paintings, sculptures, furniture, and objets d'art. An important exhibition room of drawings, engravings, and photographs complete this unique heritage ●

>> *The Carnavalet Museum*

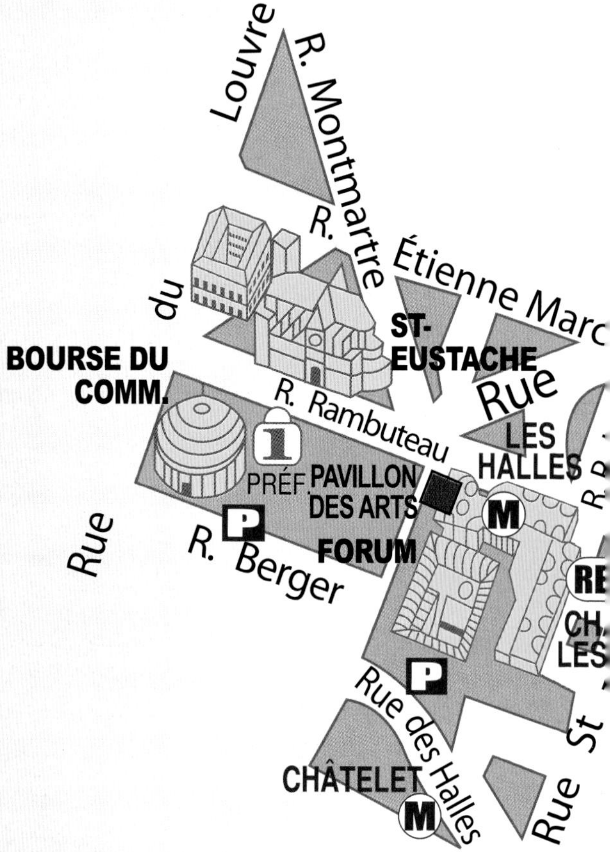

Louvre
R. Montmartre
R.
Étienne Marc
du
ST-
EUSTACHE
BOURSE DU
COMM.
Rue
R. Rambuteau
LES
HALLES
PRÉF.
PAVILLON
DES ARTS
FORUM
Rue
R. Berger
Rue des Halles
CHÂTELET
Rue St
Rue

## •8th Itinerary•

# THE «HALLES» AND POMPIDOU CENTER

ÉTIENNE MARCEL

R. aux Ours

TH. MOLIÈRE

CENTRE POMPIDOU

RAMBUTEAU

St-Martin

MUSÉE D'ART MODERNE

# 8TH ITINERARY

## THE HALLES AND POMPIDOU CENTER

The quarter of the Halles (marketplace) has a history dating back to more than one thousand years. As of the XIIth century, les **HALLES** of Paris were established on the « Champeaux », also designated as «Petits champs» (small fields) which used to be old swamps.

A few years later, Philippe-Auguste acquires the entire ownership of the lands by paying a fee to the bishopric of Paris. It is then a huge « Bazaar » whereby foodstuffs, textile, shoes, haberdashery… are sold in very special locations. Merchants settle under particular shelters close to houses where the regular businesses of manufacturers are situated. This is how the street of the Grande Friperie (secondhand clothes shops) becomes the place where secondhand clothes are traded. Progressively, other merchants start settling around those who already have their location.

Considering the increase in exchange, Philippe Auguste commands the building of the first marketplace for drapers and weavers ; however, the market continues to expand to a point whereby, as of the XVIth century, its reorganization and the enlargement of the roads are considered.

Houses are built with porticos or open galleries on the ground floor known as the « pillars of the Halles » which shall disappear during the construction of the Baltard pavilions. Due to the congestion of the Halles market, the « Halle au Blé » (wheat market) is built in 1763 on the location of the Hotel de Soisson. Until our present day, one can still distinguish the astronomical pillar of Catherine of Medicis which encloses the area of the building that has become the Bourse of Commerce.

In 1789, the cemetery of the Innocents situated amongst the streets of Saint-Denis, de la Lingerie, de la Ferronnerie and aux Fers is also fitted out into a market for flowers, fruits and vegetables.

The French Revolution, than the Empire, shall modify the urban planning of the city. The heart of Paris suffers from hygienic and security problems and questions are raised concerning the provisions of the capital.

In 1808, Napoleon I engages in a coherent reorganization of the covered markets and elaborates regulations on the slaughtering of animals. He plans to build a central marketplace between the innocents market and the wheat market.

Nevertheless, as of 1830, traffic as well as hygiene problems resurface, which prompts prefect Rambuteau to create, in 1842, the Market Commission with a mission to study the benefit of keeping the Halles at their location or move those elsewhere.

The architecture competition launched in 1848 is won by Victor Baltard who plans on building twelve pavilions covered with glass windows and cast iron small columns. Ten pavilions are built between 1852 and 1870. The construction of the last two pavilions is achieved in 1936.
The lack of available space, hemmed in by the noose of new constructions built during the renovation of the Second Empire, the saturation of traffic, hygiene problems as well as problems in the market functioning ; faced with the increase of the population in Paris, its region, in addition to an increase in their needs, all lead to the decision of relocating the Halles' wholesale market activities to Rungis and to La Villette.
The decision is taken then to create an underground scheme at the same location of the old marketplace, in order to relieve the center of Paris and open a green space. On the ground floor, the planning scheme does not voluntarily include any institutional building which could stand out as a monument, leaving this role to Saint-Eustache Church and the Bourse of Commerce, which shall become the focus of all perspectives.

Hence, the Forum of the Halles is achieved in 1986. The Halles operation constitutes the biggest masterpiece of underground urban planning ever undertaken in France, with the development of several hectares on four levels.

In the vicinity of the Forum des Halles, the **GEORGES POMPIDOU CENTER** marked the seventies with its high-tech appearance, which offers a daring contrast in the old Beaubourg quarter. Built upon a decision of President Georges Pompidou, this high place of modern and contemporary culture houses the National Museum of Modern Art, the public library of information opened to the public (BPI), exhibition galleries, movie theaters, entertainment and concert halls in addition to a research center of contemporary music (IRCAM).

The National Museum of Modern Art offers one of the most impressive collections of modern and contemporary art in the world from 1905 till our present days: Miró, Giacometti, Dubuffet, Picasso, Matisse, Léger, Chagall, Kadinsky, Warhol, Ben, César….Brancusi's studio presents a magnificent collection of works by Constantin Brancusi, major artist in the history of modern sculpture •

## •9th Itinerary•

# The butte Montmartre
# *(Hillock of Montmartre)*

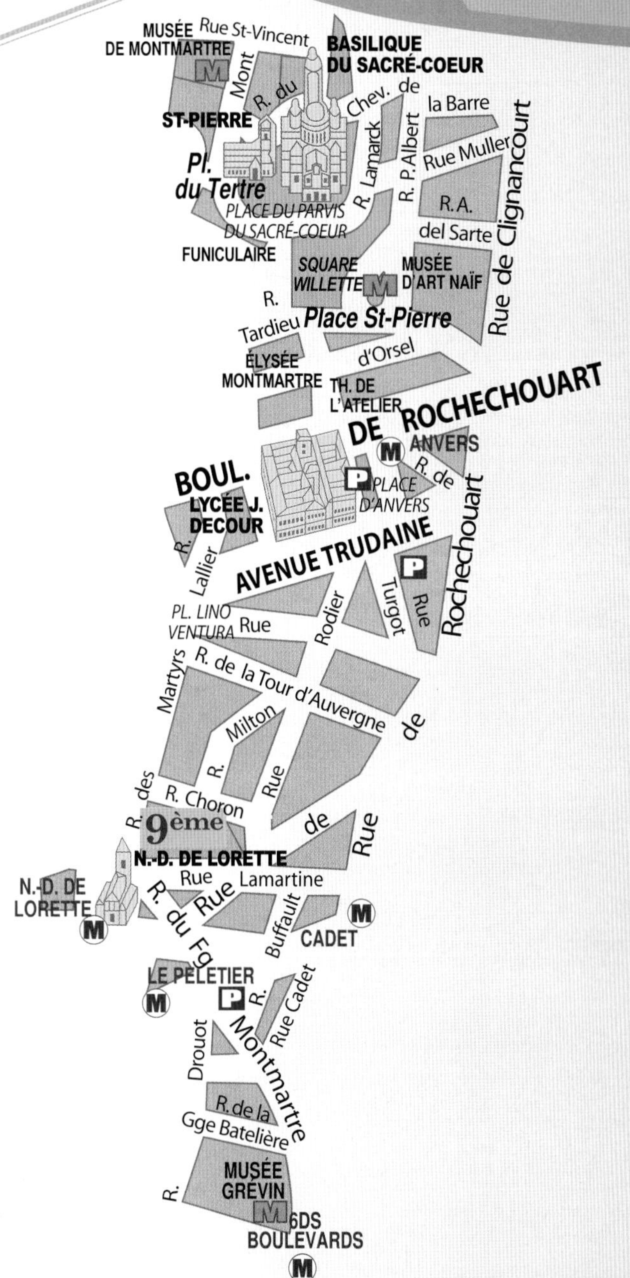
MUSÉE DE MONTMARTRE
Rue St-Vincent
BASILIQUE DU SACRÉ-COEUR
Mont
R. du
Chev. de
la Barre
ST-PIERRE
R. Lamarck
R. P. Albert
Rue Muller
Rue de Clignancourt
Pl. du Tertre
PLACE DU PARVIS DU SACRÉ-COEUR
R.A. del Sarte
FUNICULAIRE
SQUARE WILLETTE
MUSÉE D'ART NAÏF
R. Tardieu
Place St-Pierre
d'Orsel
ÉLYSÉE MONTMARTRE
TH. DE L'ATELIER
BOUL. DE ROCHECHOUART
ANVERS
R. de Rochechouart
PLACE D'ANVERS
LYCÉE J. DECOUR
R. Lallier
AVENUE TRUDAINE
Rue Turgot
Rodier
PL. LINO VENTURA
Rue
R. de la Tour d'Auvergne
Martyrs
Milton
R.
R. des
R. Choron
Rue de
de
Rue
9ème
N.-D. DE LORETTE
Rue Lamartine
R. du Fg
Rue
Buffault
CADET
LE PELETIER
R.
Rue Cadet
Drouot
Montmartre
R. de la
Gge Batelière
MUSÉE GRÉVIN
R.
GDS BOULEVARDS

COR JESU SACRATISSIMUM

## THE BUTTE MONTMARTRE
### *(HILLOCK OF MONTMARTRE)*

Situated on the large boulevards, which form a vast circle arch exceeding four kilometers, from the Bastille to the Madeleine, the **MUSÉE GRÉVIN** (Grevin Museum) is open since 1882 and pays tribute each year to the great men of this world. After recent works, 280 wax statutes-including 80 new ones-are displayed henceforth in various decors with sound effects. A novelty : it is now possible to be photographed next to your favorite star. You would also re-live the spectacular hours of the History of France through 50 personages of different epochs.

*>> The entrance of the Grévin*

The visit continues with the legendary Théâtre du Musée (Museum Theater), the meeting point of the Tout-Paris, and you would marvel at the Palais des Mirages (Mirages Palace) which never ceases to amaze people... ever since the 1900 World Fair. Finally, thanks to new light and image technologies, the « Passage à Images » takes you to a fantastic universe of transformation between illusion and reality.

*>> On the left, the dome of the Sacré-Coeur*
*>> Below, the wax statues of the Grévin museum*

Dominating this quarter, the **Butte Montmartre** (Hillock of Montmartre), at the same time a sacred hill of roman temples at the Montmartre abbey, and the political hillock of Henri IV during the Commune, has preserved its cultural and artistic identity by embracing the greatest pictorial movements of the

XIXth and XXth century (Impressionism, Cubism, Fauvism, surrealism). Montmartre is still until our present days a place of life, of historical as well as cultural discoveries, visited by more than six million visitors striving to stroll about the typical alleys of old Paris.

>> *The Montmartre Funicular*

On the tip of the hillock, the **SACRÉ-CŒUR DE MONTMARTRE** (Sacred Heart of Montmartre) is a pilgrimage church of Romano-Byzantine style.

The Sacré-Coeur basilica originates from the Catholic Church's wish of expiating « revolutionary crimes » of the insurrectionary movement of La Commune as well as washing away France's defeat during the 1870 war against Prussia.

The construction works, financed by public subscription, start in 1876 under the supervision of the architect Paul Abadie (1812-1884). The poor soil quality slows down the pace of works, which extend until 1914. Finally, the basilica is consecrated in 1919.

The basilica has an impressive nave (100 meters length on 50 meters wide) and offers the possibility of gathering masses of pilgrims.

While putting up the basilica, Abadie was inspired by the Romano-Byzantine style of Saint-Front-de-Périgueux Church, which he himself restored. The Sacré-Coeur, entirely built in white stones, comprises four domes encircling a vast cupola culminating at 94 meters. A 94 meters high bell-tower contains a large bell cast in 1895 and weighing 19 tons.

Equestrian statues of Saint-Louis and Joan of Arc surround the main façade, with its large

bronze gates. It opens onto a square that dominates Paris City and offers a magnificent view of the capital. Inside, the apse is decorated with an immense mosaic of 475 square meters designed by Luc-Olivier Merson, representing the Trinity and the devotion of France to the Sacred Heart.

Numerous statues also adorn the chapels. The Sacré-Coeur basilica is one of the most famous and most visited French monuments •

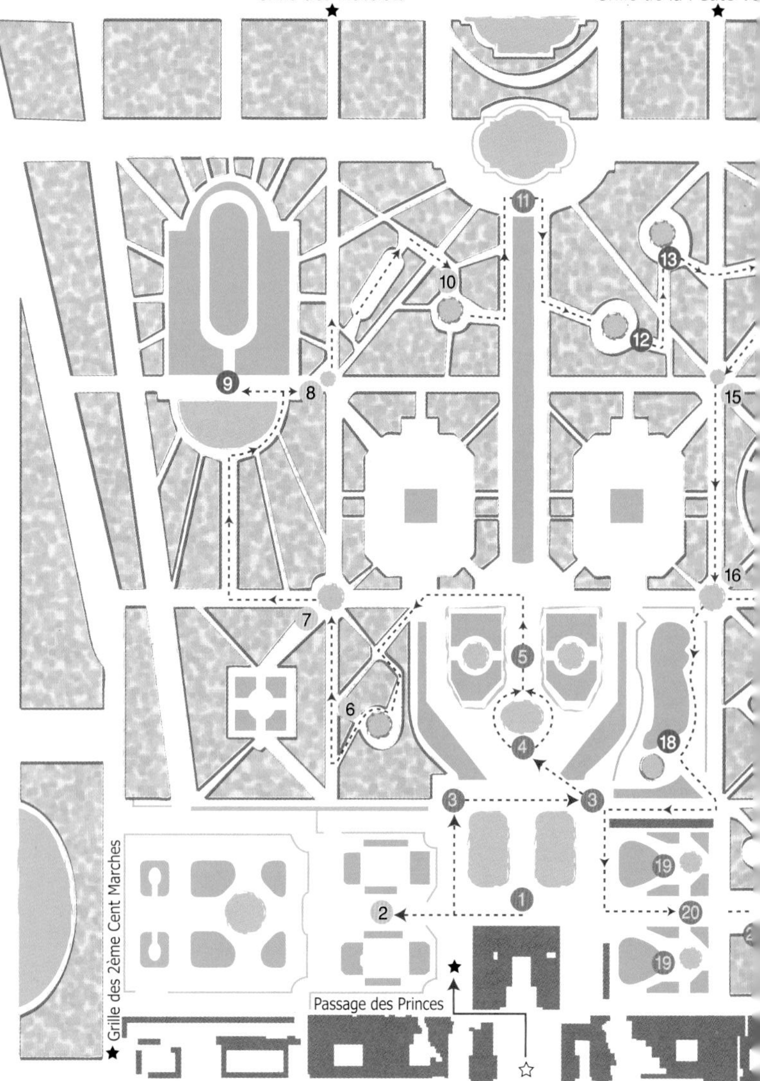
Grille des Matelots
Grille de la Petite Ve
Grille des 2ème Cent Marches
Passage des Princes
Grille d'Honneur
1
2
3
3
4
5
6
7
8
9
10
11
12
13
15
16
18
19
20
19

## The Château Versailles *(Versailles Castle)*

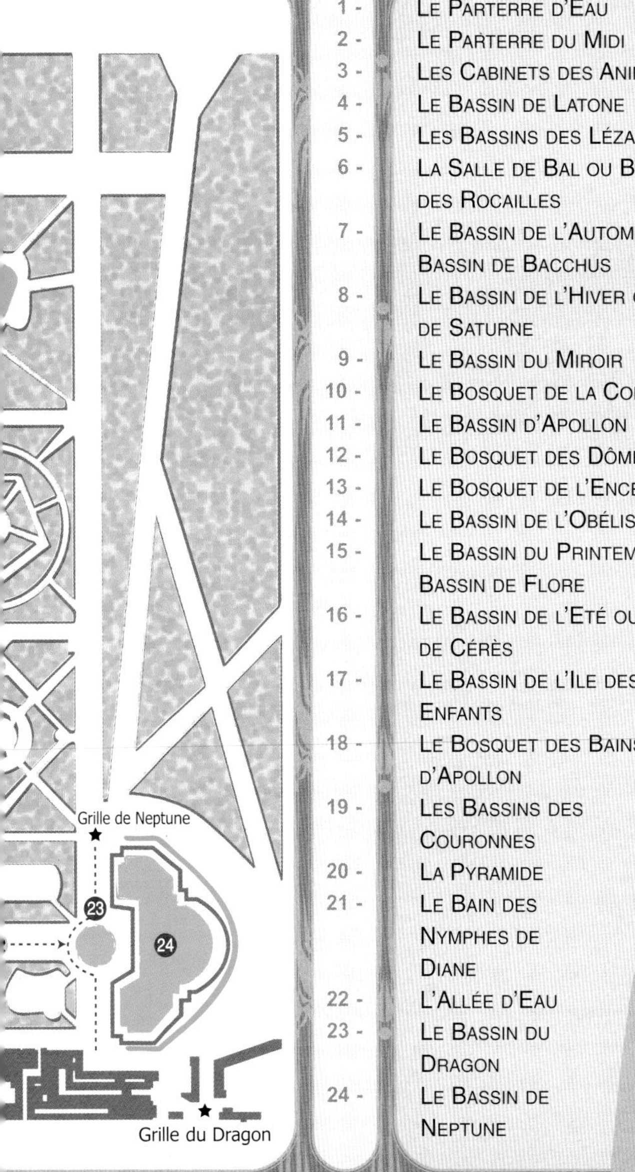


1 - Le Parterre d'Eau
2 - Le Parterre du Midi
3 - Les Cabinets des Animaux
4 - Le Bassin de Latone
5 - Les Bassins des Lézards
6 - La Salle de Bal ou Bosquet des Rocailles
7 - Le Bassin de l'Automne ou Bassin de Bacchus
8 - Le Bassin de l'Hiver ou Bassin de Saturne
9 - Le Bassin du Miroir
10 - Le Bosquet de la Colonnade
11 - Le Bassin d'Apollon
12 - Le Bosquet des Dômes
13 - Le Bosquet de l'Encelade
14 - Le Bassin de l'Obélisque
15 - Le Bassin du Printemps ou Bassin de Flore
16 - Le Bassin de l'Eté ou Bassin de Cérès
17 - Le Bassin de l'Ile des Enfants
18 - Le Bosquet des Bains d'Apollon
19 - Les Bassins des Couronnes
20 - La Pyramide
21 - Le Bain des Nymphes de Diane
22 - L'Allée d'Eau
23 - Le Bassin du Dragon
24 - Le Bassin de Neptune

# 10TH ITINERARY

## THE CHÂTEAU VERSAILLES *(VERSAILLES CASTLE)*

Each year, around ten million visitors cross the gates of the Versailles Castle, registered at the UNESCO World heritage. A Royal residence as well as a history museum, the castle is also a national palace where the Parliament sits when meeting in Congress.

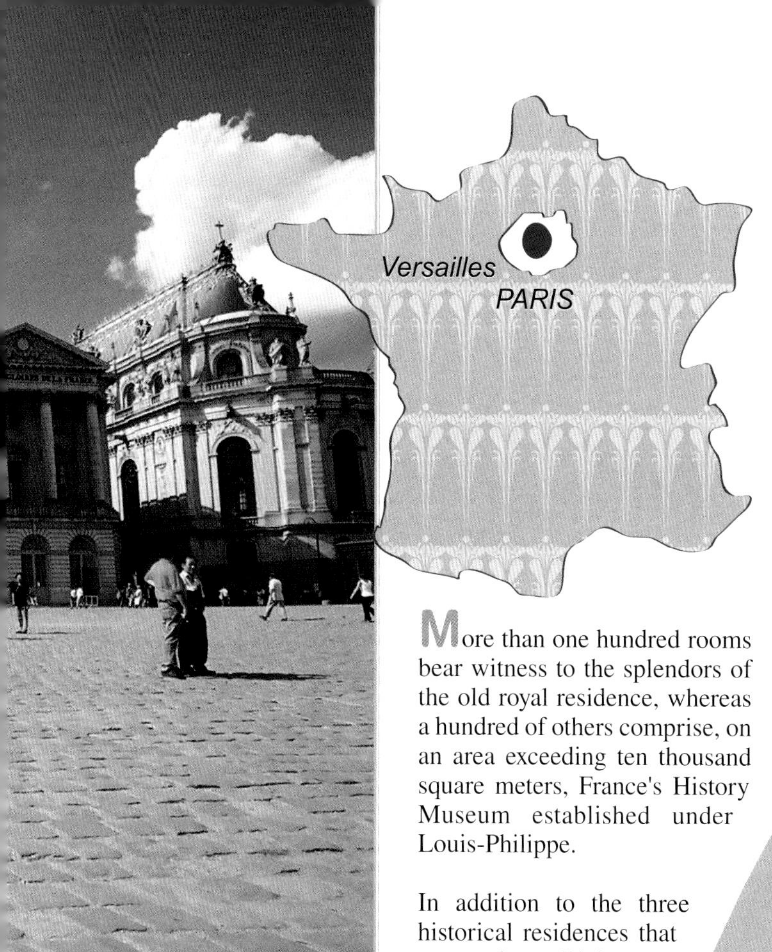


More than one hundred rooms bear witness to the splendors of the old royal residence, whereas a hundred of others comprise, on an area exceeding ten thousand square meters, France's History Museum established under Louis-Philippe.

In addition to the three historical residences that are the Château (Castle), the Grand Trianon (Big Trianon) and the Petit Trianon (Small Trianon), the Versailles estate comprises the big baroque garden drawn by Le Nôtre, the gardens of Trianon and Queen Marie-Antoinette's Hamlet as well as a wooded park situated on both sides of the Grand Canal.

Numerous constructions and outbuildings are added to the above, stretching over an area that exceeds eight hundred hectares. The Carrosses (coaches) museum at the Grande Ecurie (Big Stable) exhibits a collection of cars from the XIXth century as well as sleighs and sedan chairs of royal provenance.

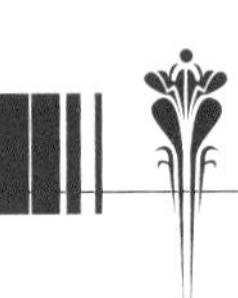

>> *The Château Neuf*

The Versailles castle also remains an important center of creation and cultural events. It features each year numerous visits-conferences, exhibitions, publications, and shows that gather major names in theater and dance in the royal Opera, the chapel or the gardens.

In parallel, services of the Senate and the National Assembly as well as the museum of the parliamentary Institution created in 1995 are established within the Castle.

>> *The pediment of one of the Château Neuf's wings*

## HISTORICAL BACKGROUND OF THE VERSAILLES CASTLE

Almost four hundred years have passed since the days of the modest residence, which King Louis XIII used to return to after his hunting days at the Castle. This symbol of the royal power is visited by three million people each year.

For four centuries, the Versailles Castle, royal residence marked by Louis XIV's seal, has undergone numerous transformations, was almost destroyed and finally became a museum.

### > *Louis XIV transforms the Castle*

While very young, Louis XIII comes hunting with his father Henri IV on the Versailles lands. He decides to build a small pavilion in 1623, where he likes to retire away from the Court. Some years later, in 1631, he entrusts Philibert le Roy to enlarge it. The tricolor building, made of bricks and stones and topped with slates, shall be qualified by Saint-Simon as a « small house of cards ».

In 1643, Louis XIV succeeds his father at five years of age. He shall not decide to carry out the first transformations of Louis XIII's castle before 1660, the year of his marriage with Marie-Therese, the Infant of Spain.

*>> The portrait of Louis XIII, by Peter Paul Rubens (1622-1625)*

Hence, from this day on, Versailles shall never cease being a vast building site, throughout the reign of the Sun King.

*>> The Statue of the Sun King (Le Roi Soleil), Louis XIV, in front of the Grand Bassin*

Whereas the design of the new castle is entrusted to the first architect Louis Le Vau, the gardens are assigned to André Le Nôtre and the decorations to Charles Le Brun. In 1668, the project of enlarging the castle from the garden side by a « stone envelope » is adopted.
Four years later, in 1672, the works of the « Appartement des Bains » (Baths Apartment) and the Ambassadors escalator are undertaken.
A new modification is carried out on the initiative of Jules-Hardouin Mansart : in 1678, the terrace on the gardens is suppressed and replaced by the Mirror Gallery.
Le Nôtre conceives the vast and fabulous park. This titanic work is achieved between 1661 and 1700. Groves, channels and flower-beds stand out from the ground, adorned with marble, bronze or lead statues as well as basins animated with fountains.

*>> The dome of the Château de Versailles Chapel*

On May 6, 1682, King Louis XIV solemnly announces that he shall install the government of France at Versailles.
Thus, Versailles becomes the political capital but also the know-how showcase of French artists and artisans.
With the passing years, the Castle goes through various modifications. The Southern wing (1678-1682), then the Northern wing (1685-1689), the Trianon and the Chapel, which was achieved in 1710, all come into being. Upon the king's death, on September 1st, 1715, the Castle is nothing but a vast masonry abandoned by the courtiers. This shall only last during the Regency.
When Louis XV reaches adulthood in 1722, he returns to Versailles and the Court settles there until the Revolution.
Transformations and modifications are once again the fate of the palace. The apartments of the King, the Queen and the Princes are redecorated according to the taste of that era. Unfortunately, the Baths apartment and the Ambassadors escalator are destroyed ; however, the Salon Hercule, the Opera and the Petit Trianon are created.

### > *The Château musée (Castle museum)*

Louis XVI finishes the Queen's Hamlet in 1783. As of the beginning of the Revolution, on October 6, 1789, the royal family leaves Versailles for Paris. Louis XVI shall not have enough time to carry out the projects he had deeply reflected upon for the Castle. The furniture is sold during a public auction. Paintings, antiques, and gems are transported to the Louvre. The National Library receives the books and medals.

Plans of Versailles and Paris in 1789.

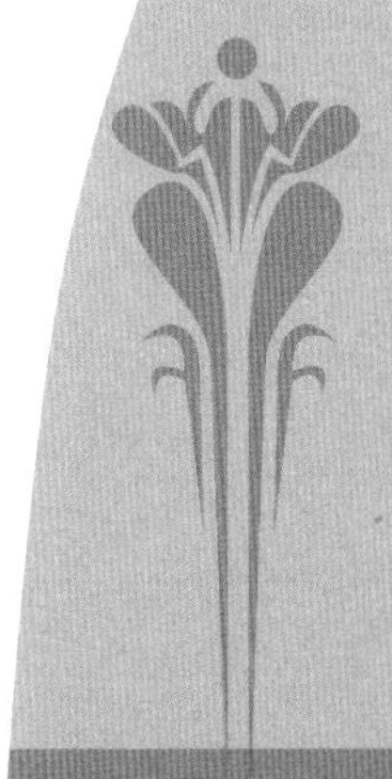

>> The portrait of king Louis Philippe

The Republic keeps the Castle. It shall house a small room of natural history, a library, a music conservatory, as well as a « special Museum of the French school ».

When the Empire is proclaimed, Versailles becomes once again the Crown residence. Napoleon I undertakes the restoration works and wishes to reside there during the summer season. History shall prevent him from making this wish come true.
As for his successors to the throne of France, Louis XVIII and Charles X, brothers of Louis XVI, they shall not have any interest in moving back to Versailles.

Threatened of destruction in 1830, the Castle is « saved » by Louis-Philippe who transforms it into a museum, inaugurated in 1837, and dedicated to « All the glories of France » in a spirit of national reconciliation.
The implementation of this museum causes the destruction of the majority of the princes and the courtiers' apartments, namely those situated at both wings of the Castle.
Transformed into a military hospital during the 1870 war, the Castle shall become the siege of the Prussians' military and political staff headquarters. The German Empire shall be proclaimed in 1871 in the Mirror Gallery.

The Commune events lead to the French government settling at Versailles. Thus, on January 30, 1875, the republic is proclaimed at the Opera Hall where the National Assembly has its seat.

## VISIT OF THE CASTLE

### > The King's Grand Apartment

« And since the Sun is the motto of the King, seven planets were picked to serve as the paintings' theme in the seven rooms of this

apartment » (Felibien, 1674). This Grand Apartment consecrates the glory of the Sun King. As a continuation of the Abundance lounge, the Venus, then the Diane, Mars, Mercury and at last Apollo lounges are each devoted to a star. Therefore, during the construction of the château neuf (new castle), it is named the Planets apartment. In 1710 a new hall is added, this time devoted to a mythology hero : it is the Hercules lounge. It is designed to host the Lunch at Simon de Veronese, offered by the Republic of Venice to Louis XIV in 1664 (restoration in 1997). It competes with the Glass Gallery because of the opulence of its marble décor, the quality of the chimney's chiseled bronze (the most beautiful of the castle). The ceiling, masterpiece of the painter Francois Lemoyne who achieves it between 1733 and 1736, where Hercules' Apotheosis is represented, has also been restored.

*-> On the left, the king's room*

## > The Mirror gallery : to the glory of the King

Versailles' masterpiece, the Mirror gallery, is set up in 1678, when Versailles becomes the official residence. It drastically changes the order of the Planets' apartment. After the Nimegue peace treaty which marks the culminating point of the reign, Louis XIV commands Le Brun to represent the good deeds of his government on the gallery's vault. The first Painter conceives thirty paintings surrounded by stuccos : the sovereign appears like a roman emperor, grand administrator of his kingdom and conqueror of foreign powers.

The gallery is 73 meters long, 10.50 meter large and 12.30 meters high. It is completed on the northern side by the War lounge and on the southern side by the Peace Lounge. Seventeen windows opening onto the garden match the seventeen arcades adorned with mirrors. These mirrors, of an exceptional dimension, were achieved by a Parisian manufacture created by Colbert to compete with the products of Venice. The arcades are separated by marble pilasters with gilded bronze capitals ornamented with fleur-de-lis and French cockerels, according to the new « French » order invented by Le Brun.

## > The Queen's Chamber

It is still in the same state as it was when Marie-Antoinette left Versailles in 1789. The rococo style panelling as well as the ceiling painted by Francois Boucher (1703-1770) were ordered by Louis XV towards 1730 to please his wife Marie Leszczinska. Marie-Antoinette finds all this outdated ; she endeavors to renew all the furniture and namely the silk fabrics weaved or embroidered with lilac and peacock feathers, that lined the recess and the huge imperial bed (restoration in 1976).

>> *The Queen's room*

## LTHE TRIANON AND QUEEN'S HAMLET CASTLES

Trianon is the name of a small village which origin goes back to the Middle Age. In 1660, Louis XIV buys the lands and links them to the Versailles estate.

### > THE GRAND TRIANON

Situated on the Trianon village site that Louis XIV razed, the current palace was preceded by a first castle built by Louis Le Vau in 1670, named porcelain Trianon due to its decoration with blue Faience (earthenware). It fell into ruin and was replaced by the Grand Trianon in 1687-1688, built by Jules Hardouin-Mansart. An Italian style one-floor building surmounted by a balustrade that used to be ornamented by sculptures, it was composed of two wings linked up by a peristyle.

Entirely marked by pink marble columns and pilasters, the reason behind his designation as marble Trianon, it was Louis XIVth country residence. The King's chamber was at first set up in the left wing, then as of 1703 in the right wing, next to Madam de Maintenon's apartments. With the Grand Dauphin occupying the old chamber of the king, the royal family resided in the Trianon-sous-Bois wing, the only part of the building to have a floor as of 1705.

Somewhat neglected in the XVIIIth century, although it was occupied by the queen Marie Leszczinska then refurnished by Louis XV and Madame de Pompadour, the Grand Trianon was granted by Napoleon to his mother in 1805, then the Emperor himself inhabited it in 1810. Louis-Philippe reshapes it a last time for his family in 1836-1838. On this occasion, the chapel is built, decorated of paintings from the XIXth century. A last chamber was fitted out in 1845 for the queen of the Belgians, daughter of the king.

Official residence of the Presidents of Republic since General de Gaulle, the Grand Trianon-having preserved its Louis XIV epoch panelling-was refurnished during the sixties with furniture from the Empire and Louis-Philippe epochs, as for the paintings ordered by Louis XIV, they recovered their locations. Inspired by the Ovide Metamorphoses, they deal with mythological subjects (History of Hercules, Io, and Minerva), illustrating the names of Le Brun's students : Verdier, Houasse, La Fosse, Coypel, Jouvenet.

Numerous foreign guests were received by France at the Grand Trianon : queens of England and the Netherlands, the Shah of Iran, American presidents Carter and Reagan, Russian presidents Gorbatchev and Eltsine.

## > The Petit Trianon (Small Trianon)

In order to complete the composition of the French Garden, the Pompadour marchioness suggests to Louis XV the construction of this small castle, which façade is inspired by that of Trianon-sous-Bois.

Built from 1761 to 1768 by Ange-Jacques Gabriel, the Petit Trianon features an original plan. Due to the topography of the land, its kitchens, though situated in the underground, they level up with the honor staircase. Moving tables destined to serve the first floor halls have been provided for, but were not achieved. The Chapel was not done before 1774.

This is where Louis XV cultivated his taste for botany ; he even constituted a library on this theme. Madam Du Barry was the first to fully benefit from this new castle. Upon the King's death in 1774, Louis XVI offered it to his wife Marie-Antoinette. The latter lived as a simple chatelaine in this setting, far away from the Court, surrounded by her friends the Ladies de Polignac and de Lamballe.

Playing excessively the billiard, backgammon, loosing a lot of money, she builds a theater where she performs in plays by Sedaine or Beaumarchais. Also, seeking isolation, she installs sliding mirrors in front of her boudoir's windows, a former Louis XV coffee hall. The gardens were her constant concern. As of 1774, she undertakes the creation of the Anglo Chinese garden, where she organizes sumptuous parties for passing sovereigns, her brother Joseph II, emperor of Germany, Gustave III, King of Sweden.

Under the Empire, the Petit Trianon was the residence of Pauline Borghese, sister of Napoleon, then the Empress Marie-Louise. In 1867, Empress Eugenie gathers an art collection that belonged to Marie-Antoinette, which marked the starting of the myth fostered around the Queen.

### > *Le Hameau de la reine Marie Antoinette*

The taste for nature, developed in England, became very fashionable in France due to Jean-Jacques Rousseau. The queen wanted to have her own village where she could play the role of a shepherdess. Richard Mique built the Hamlet between 1783 and 1785, seeking inspiration from the drawings of painter Hubert Robert. Twelve cottages were originally disposed around the Grand Lac (three were razed). The queen possessed her own house, linked by a wooden gallery to the billiard on top of which Mique fitted himself out an apartment. On the staircase, saint-Clement earthenware flower pots were placed with the queen's monogram. The farm, where the queen received her milk from, was situated a little aside. This milk was served at the cleanness Creamery, at the bottom of the Pêcherie (Fishery) tower or the Marlborough tower, first construction of the Hamlet.

Although the close friends invited by Marie-Antoinette in this small village enjoyed playing the role of shepherds, they were also delighted by the utmost luxury. The Barn (destroyed) served as ball room, there was also a Boudoir next to the Queen's House.

Several planned constructions were not achieved : the solitude pavilion, an artificial ruin as well as a vast rectangular basin.

Under the Empire, the Hamlet was refurnished for Empress Marie-Louise.

# THE VERSAILLES AND TRIANON GARDENS

The Versailles Park is the archetype of a regular garden built according to a rigorous and geometric architectural design. The essential principle consists in clearing the palaces' accesses to combine the garden's geometry with the architectural lines. The tree clumps, moved to the back, become the remote frame of a largely open perspective.

The Versailles and Trianon estate is composed of three distinct parts :

~ The garden.

~ The groves, which constitute transition architectures between the flower-beds and big trees covering the horizon. They constitute a place for taking a walk and for recreation.

~ The forest, cleared by large rectilinear paths and star shaped crossroads, is fitted out for hunting and shooting.

## > THE GARDEN

Louis XIV is fond of the Versailles gardens as much as he is of the Castle if not more. Up until his death, he personally presides over their fitting-out, takes walk therein very often, and this where he accompanies his distinguished guests and foreign ambassadors.
In 1661, he commissions André Le Nôtre (1623-1700) to create and manage the gardens. Works are carried out just before the enlargement building sites of Louis XIII's palace. This titanic enterprise shall last around forty years.

Louis XIV uses the gardens to organize sumptuous feasts and towards the end of his life, he elaborates an itinerary through which he indicates the « Way to show the Versailles gardens ».

André Le Nôtre was not working alone : Jean-Baptiste Colbert (1619-1683) manages the whole planning ; Charles Le Brun (1619-1690) provides the drawings of numerous statues and fountains ; a little later, Jules Hardouin-Mansart commands decors that are more and more sober, he also builds the first orangery of Le Vau while duplicating it. At last, the King himself asks that all projects be submitted to him personally and requires the « tiniest details ».

The creation of the gardens entails an unequalled load of work at that epoch. Enormous soil cartages are necessary to fit out the flower-beds, the Orangery, the basins, the Canal, where nothing existed but woods, meadows and swamps. The soil is transported in wheelbarrows, trees are transported on carts from all the provinces of France ; thousands of men, sometimes entire regiments participated in this vast undertaking.

The Versailles Gardens, a true plant-like architecture that prolongs the lines and perspectives of the Castle, were created with the aim of combining art and nature. Built according to a rigorous and geometric architectural planning, they are organized around two axes which intersect at right angles at the level of the terrace, thus dominating vast perspectives :

~ the north-south axis from the Neptune basin until the Swiss water hall.

~ the east-west axis from the façade of the Mirror Gallery until the end of the Grand Canal. This is Versailles' major perspective which Le Nôtre opened up to infinity. It attracts the sight to the horizon and measures 3200 meters, from the castle's façade to the Park's gate.

### > The Groves

Also named greenery halls, the Versailles groves served as open air salons concealed in the heart of wooded spaces inside the small park, from Louis XIV's epoch up until the end of the Old regime.

As an integral part of the Versailles gardens, the groves are used alternately as : halls, exhibition rooms, theaters, galleries. The basins were also qualified as mirrors, carpets, embroideries. Some groves were equipped with buffets, tables and even plant ceilings.

Thus, a real open air castle was built as an extension to the stone castle.

The groves were a place of feasting and entertainment where Louis XIV could indulge his taste in games and shows.

Today, only five out of the fourteen groves are in a good state of preservation and open to the public.

## > The Grand Trianon Gardens

Although they have no symbolic solar meaning as the Versailles gardens, the Grand Trianon Gardens must have had an essential role in Louis XIV's view. Open from all sides, this « Flore palace » had to integrate in the tamed nature of the park « à la française », drawn by the gardener Le Bouteux, nephew of Le Nôtre.

Two flower-beds successively rise in tiers : the High Garden punctuated by two basins adorned with kids by Girardon ; the Lower Graden with a basin decorated by Marsy. The central axis leads to the flat bottom ornamented with dragons by Hardy.

On the right side, a small wood stretches out, with the Buffet d'Eau at its entry, built by Hardouin-Mansart in 1703 at the site of the first Trianon's cascade. It is the sole basin with a mythological theme in this garden, ornamented with sculptures by Mazière, Poirier, Le Lorrain, Hardy and Van Clève, with Neptune and Amphitrite as a central theme. The return path to the Trianon-sous-Bois wing is done via the Green Hall followed by a flower-bed surmounted by the Antiques Hall, adorned with busts. The « Jardin des Sources » (Sources Garden), which preceded the English parks of the XVIIIth century, used to stretch out between the Gallery and this wing, it is disfigured today. Finally, behind the right wing, the King's Garden appears ; a private garden decorated with a basin by Tuby. On the Grand Canal's side, at the bottom of the Mirror Lounge, the king had planted orange trees in the soil.

Louis XIV wanted this garden to be adorned with the rarest flowers. Hyacinths, wallflowers, veronicas, carnations, lilies and rose campions emitted such strong perfumes that the king, according to Saint-Simon's saying, had to leave his garden one of these days. Le Bouteux had put in place a planting system in pots that allowed a swift change of the clumps. Around one million pots were necessary to decorate this garden with flowers, even during winter.

## > The French Garden

Louis XV settled in the Grand Trianon and, urged by Madam de Pompadour, he decided to build a menagerie, a small farm with cows, sheep, and poultry, surrounded by vegetable gardens and orchards, which foreshadowed Marie-Antoinette's Hamlet. The architect Ange-Jacques Gabriel attached a garden to it with constructions to taste the harvested produce. In 1749-1750 the French Pavilion was built, then the Fresh Lounge in 1753. Lattice

work added a touch of great value to the decoration of this small garden, hollowed out with a basin named Evergreen.

The layout of the French Garden was progressively put in order by the gardener Belleville. Its completion coincided with the construction of the Petit Trianon from 1761 to 1768. Developing his taste for botany and agriculture, Louis XV commanded the installation of warm greenhouses and the planting of some rare flowers and plants such as pineapple and coffee trees, cactus, cultivated by the gardeners Claude and Antoine Richard and designed by Jussieu. As of 1774, the creation of the Anglo Chinese Park by Marie-Antoinette unfortunately made the king's botanical garden disappear.

Under Napoleon, the Grand Trianon was linked to the French Garden by a small bridge striding over a hollow path.

### > *The English Garden*

Wishing to have her country house, Marie-Antoinette has Louis XVI offer her the Petit Trianon. As of 1774, she calls upon the architect Richard Mique whose first undertaking is to create a « jeu de bagues » with a gallery at the stern of the castle, on the site of Louis XV's botanical garden (1776).

Having surrounded herself with the counseling of the Count of Caraman, well supported by her architect, by her intendant Bonnefoy du Plan and by her gardener Claude Richard, the queen proceeds to enormous earthworks to create a garden with an Anglo Chinese style, very fashionable at that epoch, punctuated with « manufactures ». Following the examples set by the Marquis de Girardin at the Ermenonville Castle as well as the Duke of Orleans at the Park Monceau in Paris, Marie-Antoinette successively commissions the building of the Temple de l'Amour (Love Temple) (1778), which she could oversee from her room at the Petit Trianon, the Grotto and the Salon du Rocher (Rock Lounge) or Belvedere (1778-1779). These constructions are established on rocks and artificial islets, in the midst of which a river flows. Far off, around the Grand Lake, the queen finishes her project by building the Hamlet from 1783 to 1785, which is a small dream village designed in the taste of an enchanting nature.

## CULTURAL PROGRAMS

- To the visits-conferences and the visits-workshops (destined more specifically to a young public), music conferences are added as well as an ambitious cultural policy through shows and animations.
- The Automne Musical (Musical Fall) of the Versailles Castle, organized by Versailles' Baroque music Center features concerts and baroque operas.
- Musical Thursdays of the royal Chapel, organized by Versailles' Baroque music Center.
- The « Grandes Eaux Musicales », from April to October as well as the nightly Grandes Eaux in July.
- The night Festivals, on the Neptune basin, in August and September.
- Furthermore, temporary exhibitions are regularly organized. We can cite among others « Les Tables Royales », « Topkapi in Versailles », « Jean-Marc Nattier », « Madam de Pompadour and Arts », « the Oudry animals ». In 2004, the Versailles Castle presented « the reign of Kang Xi », « Houdon, lights sculptor », and « Maurice Quentin de La Tour, the souls thief ».

## THE CARROSSES MUSEUM (COACH MUSEUM)

Established since 1985 at the Grande Ecurie (Big Stable) of Versailles Castle, the Carrosses museum gathers a cars collection constituted by king Louis-Philippe and destined to be part of the museum dedicated to « All the glories of France ». These cars mostly date back to the XIXth century.

The vaulted gallery of the Grande Ecurie allows you to discover coaches dating back to the marriage of Napoleon I, seven gala cars of the imperial court, the coronation coach of Charles X, the funeral cart of Louis XVIII.
The only ones left from the Old Regime are : six sleighs, sedan chairs, and the Dauphin's coach which was the property of the Dauphin Louis of France (Louis XVII) who died in 1789.

During the Revolution, more than 2000 cars occupied the royal stables.

## PRACTICAL VERSAILLES

### >> How to access the Versailles Castle

*SNCF :* Versailles Chantiers *(departure Paris : Montparnasse).*
Versailles right bank *(departure Paris : Saint-Lazare).*

*RER :* Versailles left bank *(departure Paris: line C).*

*Bus :* 171 stops at Versailles Armes square *(departure : Sèvres bridge).*

***Parking :*** bus and cars : Armes square, Petite Venise, (Grand canal) Grand Trianon ; Petit Trianon.

### >> Practical information

***The Castle :***
open every day except on Mondays and certain public holidays, or during official ceremonies.
-April 1st-October 31st : 9:00am-18:30 *(last admission : 18:00).*
-November 1st-March 31st : 9:00am-17:30 *(last admission : 17:00).*

***The Grand Trianon and the Petit Trianon :***
open every day except on certain public holidays.
-April 1st-October 31st :12:00am-18:30 *(last admission : 18:00).*
-November 1st-March 31st : 12:00am-17h30 *(last admission : 17:00).*

***The Carrosses museum :***
open only on Saturdays and Sundays during the summer season.
***Information on 01 30 83 77 88.***

***The Versailles Garden and the groves :***
Admission fee during the high season : from April 1st till October 31st, from 9:00 am to 18:30.
Free access after 18:30. Free access from November to March.

***The grand Park*** :
is accessible to vehicles through the Queen's gate, the Matelos (sailors) gate and the Porte Saint-Antoine *(opening hours : 8:00am in winter, 7:00am in summer, and closing hours at the sunset).*
***Telephone : 01 30 83 77 88.***
***Internet site : http:://www.chateauversailles.fr***

## 11TH ITINERARY

### DISNEYLAND RESORT PARIS

Disneyland Resort Paris, the number one vacation destination in Europe with more than 12 million visitors per year, offers you an enchanting experience in a magical world.

In this timeless place, full of magic, kids and elderly people will share strong sensations, lots of fun and thrilling experiences in the Disneyland Park, Walt Disney Studios Park, and Disney Village.

# the Disney Parks

## The Disneyland Park
### « enter into a fairy tale universe... »

The Disneyland Park celebrates adventurous spirit, the passion of the imaginary and the pleasures of discovery. This 56 hectares park offers around forty attractions and shows, parades, encounters with famous Disney characters, à la carte or self service restaurants, as well as a range of shops with magical settings. Discover this park with its sumptuous decoration where you will be transported into a world of enchantment and excitement.

## The Walt Disney Studios Park
### « Welcome to the magical backstage world ! »

Situated next to the Disneyland Park, the Walt Disney Studios Park offers visitors a full day of attractions and constitutes an interactive discovery of the « backstage » of cinema as well as animation, and television. Designed in the aspect of a real cinema studio, the park comprises four « production zones », spectacular attractions and new shows. A true glimpse of the behind the scene world coupled with a breathtaking leap into the heart of action !

## Disney Village

The ultimate themed leisure district, which links Disneyland Park to the Hotels of the site, Disney Village offers guests the chance to indulge in entertainment : restaurants and bars, a night-club, boutiques, a permanent show : Buffalo Bill's Wild West Show, a Gaumont Multiplex with 15 cinema screens. Disney Village is one of the biggest entertainment poles of the Parisian region ; it mostly attracts people because of the succession of new shows, street entertainment, live concerts and music festivals such as the Latina Festival or the Celtic Festival.

## The Seven Disney Hotels

Situated a few steps away from the Theme Parks and Disney Village, the seven Disney Hotels (Disneyland Hotel, Disney's Hotel New York, Disney's Newport Bay Club, Disney's Sequoia Lodge, Disney's Hotel Cheyenne, Disney's Hotel Santa Fe and Disney's Davy Crockett Ranch) allow visitors to further enjoy the entertainment and the dream world, to live the magic day and night while benefiting from exclusive advantages such as free shuttle services to the Parks, free parking, the Disney Express service which is in charge of luggage transfer from the train to the hotel, the Disney Boutiques or even visit of the Disney Characters. These enchanted places take you to a dream world thanks to their varied themes.

## The Golf Disneyland

Located a few kilometers from the Disney Parks, the Golf Disneyland is open all year round, seven days a week. It offers golfers a 27-hole course.
The course is suitable for players of all levels, from amateur to professional. The architect, Ronald Fream, gave the long par 5 « double fairways » for a better graduation in the difficulties. Hence, experienced golfers will always find new challenges to meet, while amateurs need not be put off by insurmountable obstacles.

## Disney's Ranch Davy Crockett « a trappers village in the heart of a 57 hectares forest »

A holiday destination of its own, Disney's Ranch Davy Crockett is a trappers village, open all year round to Disney Parks visitors as well as to families eager to benefit from a stay in a natural surrounding, in the heart of an oak forest : private bungalows made of wooden logs, tropical swimming pool, sports and educational activities, workshops for children and live parties are planned for you to unwind in this charming environment •

NOTE

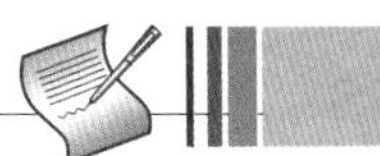

NOTE

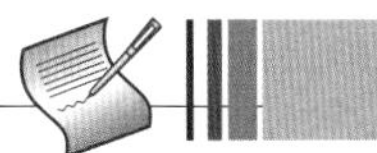

# NOTE

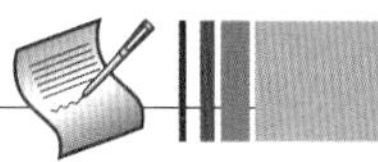

# NOTE

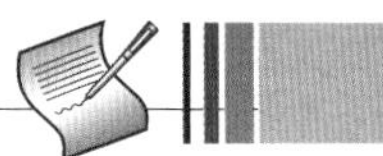

# NOTE

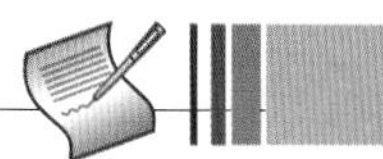

# NOTE

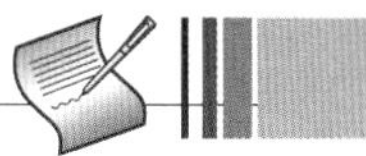

TEXTS, PICTURES, CONCEPTION, LAYOUT AND REPRODUCTION ARE TOTALLY DEVISED BY

**PARAVISION®**,

with the exception of the texts and photos of pages 156, 157, 160, 161, 162, 163, 164, 165, 166, 167, 168, 169, 170, 171, 172, 173,174, 175, 176 and 177 ©Château de Versailles, with the most kind authorization of the press relations department of the Château de Versailles, and of the texts and photos of pages 178, 179 and 180 Disneyland® Resort Paris, with the most kind authorization of the department « relations presse produit » of Disneyland® Resort Paris